Endorsements

Merging the revelatory anthropology of René Girard with the creation philosophy of Alfred Whitehead is a romance that needed to be written! And Andre Rabe has done just that, achieving a theological breakthrough while bringing urgently needed springtime to Girardian mimetic theory. Rabe's work is a profound, moving, lucid synthesis of two of the seminal thinkers of the modern era. A truly vital contemporary work of anthropological theology!

> —**Anthony Bartlett**, Ph.D, Theologian, philosopher and founder of the Bethany Center for Nonviolent Theology and Spirituality, author of *Signs of Change, The Bible's Evolution of Divine Nonviolence*

The explosive work of Alfred North Whitehead and René Girard continue to inspire distinctive trajectories of research and application, from the sciences, to philosophy, theology, and religion. Writing with both clarity and conviction, Andre Rabe's work is at the cutting edge of growing interest in metaphysics and mimesis and their relationship to each other.

> —**Andrew M. Davis**, Ph.D., Program Director of the Center for Process Studies, author of *Metaphysics of Exo-Life: Toward a Constructive Whiteheadian Cosmotheology*

Andre Rabe does a masterful job of bringing together two of the most important and influential thinkers of the last century. The result is a promising proposal for how to think well in our current age. Get this book!

> —**Thomas Jay Oord**, Ph. D., Director of the Center for Open and Relational Theology, author of *Pluriform Love: An Open and Relational Theology of Well-Being*

With Rabe's ambidextrous approach (Whitehead-informed metaphysics on the one hand and Girard-informed anthropology on the other), the world has been gifted something unique and, in turn, has had its overall uniqueness increased! I'm so excited this book is a reality. It is my new go-to-resource for all things living at the intersection of process theology and psychoanalytic desire.

—**Jonathan J. Foster**, Th.D., author of Theology of Consent: Mimetic Theory in an Open and Relational Universe

Rabe's groundbreaking work moves the philosopher Whitehead's metaphysics of beauty, creativity and freedom into deep dialogue with Girard's anthropological approach to the human predicament so that each of these major thinkers offers a corrective and complement of the other. By meticulously analyzing and revisiting Girard's concept of mimetic desire through Whitehead's categories, this highly original and creative study provides a detailed blueprint for moving forward with constructive interpretations of mimetic desire and Girard's work. At the same time, Rabe shows how Girard's anthropology practically grounds Whitehead's speculative metaphysics in an historical way, showing surprising congruences in their thought. Essential reading for anyone interested in constructive Girardian possibilities or deeper understanding of either of these two giants of the 20th century.

—**Rebecca Adams**, Independent Scholar and Freelance Academic Editor, Member of The Colloquium on Violence and Religion, and former Managing Editor of the Journal of Religion and Literature at the University of Notre Dame

Processing Mimetic Reality

Harmonizing Alfred North Whitehead and René Girard

By ANDRE RABE

SacraSage

Paperback: 978-1-958670-21-7
Hardcover: 978-1-958670-22-4
e-book: 978-1-958670-23-1

Printed in the United States of America

Library of Congress Cataloguing-in-Publication Data
Processing Mimetic Reality: Harmonizing Alfred North Whitehead and René Girard /
Andre Rabe

Table of Contents

TABLE OF CONTENTS

Acknowledgements

The book first took shape in the form of my doctoral dissertation. Dr. Thomas Oord, whose broad-minded approach inspires conversation across multiple disciplines, such as theology, science, and philosophy, acted as my dissertation advisor. Dr. Anthony Bartlett, who has pushed the boundaries of Girardian scholarship and opened new possibilities of meaning in the process, was on the defense committee. And so was Dr. Andrew Davis, whose ability to make process philosophy relevant and clear is a rare gift indeed. I have not only been enriched by their scholarship but have also enjoyed the privilege of their friendship.

What a joy it has been to make the acquaintance of Girardian scholar Rebecca Adams. She was the first to engage Girard on the theme of positive mimesis. During the review process, her insights, encouragement, and keen eye for detail were invaluable. She gave of herself and her time so generously. I look forward to our conversations continuing.

The ideas explored in this work have formed over decades; consequently, the people who have influenced these thoughts are innumerable. However, some stand out because of the consistency and beauty of their influence: Mary-Anne, my fellow adventurer in thought and life, who patiently and persistently questions ideas until their relevance to life become clear; Our students, whose weekly conversations and comments open so many new perspectives. I gratefully acknowledge you as co-creators of these ideas.

1

A New Synthesis in Process and Mimetic Theory

We're all in the process of making sense of our reality. Finding ourselves in an environment already filled with symbols, meanings, and stories, we naturally join in this meaning-making activity. We have moments of clarity on this journey in which the complex narratives that flood our world make sense. Contrasts find harmony, chaos finds a pattern, fragments find their place in the whole, scattered symbols find their sequence within a larger story, and we see our part in this unfolding beauty.

Two exceptional thinkers who can help us find such moments of clarity are the French academic René Girard (1923-2015) and the British philosopher Alfred North Whitehead (1861-1947). Some would consider Whitehead and Girard unlikely conversational partners. After all, Girard is known for his anthropological theory, and Whitehead is generally known for his metaphysics. However, I intend to show that deep, broad, and significant harmonies can be developed between process philosophy and mimetic theory. Harmonizing these two thought frameworks can transform the way we create meaning and enrich our experience.

René Girard

Girard's mimetic theory begins with a central insight into the nature of human desire. Consciously, we consider ourselves the authors of our desires, but unconsciously desires are formed by our imitative/reflective relationships with others. From there, his narrative explanation expands, exploring the processes that made us human, including the development of symbolic thought, the evolution of culture and religion, and the dramatic way the biblical narrative subverts the meaning of the symbols that shaped us.

Mimetic desire, the unconscious way in which humans reflect the desires of others, shapes us individually but also communally, socially, and culturally. Girard recognized that desire does not erupt spontaneously between a person and the object of desire. Rather the movement of desire is triangular. Humans connect intimately with the interiority of others who are like them. And when we recognize in others what we think we lack in ourselves, they become models ... unconsciously. Consequently, their desires become our desires and the triangular movement is set in motion between subject, model, and object of desire. This mimetic capacity intensifies our ability to love... and to do violence. Girard does not sugar-coat the darker side of human development but acknowledges our capacity for both good and evil. He insists that we look at what we prefer to ignore. Humans have natural biases, blind spots produced by the very processes that made us human. For him, becoming human wasn't a smooth transition from animalistic violence to greater rationality. Instead, violence increased in proportion to our increased mental capacities. However, humans invented an ingenious way of controlling violence, making religion and civilization possible.

Girard recognizes the positive aspects of mimesis but primarily develops his theory around the conflictual/violent elements.[1] He explicitly acknowledged this focus on the negative: "Thus, in my work, the 'bad' mimesis is always dominant, but the 'good' one is of course even more important."[2] This emphasis on the negative has understandably cast the mold for Girardian scholarship. Some have even suggested that his ideas constitute an ontology of violence.[3] Girard himself considered such an interpretation to be mistaken.[4] Nevertheless, the emphasis on the negative side of mimesis remains predominant in Girardian scholarship.

Good mimesis is an underdeveloped area I intend to address in this present work, which "is of course even more important." Girard acknowledged the transformative effect of the revelation of Christ on human history, but for much of his career he eschewed the theological aspects.[5] I will show instead that mimetic theory gives us a realistic understanding of our past, can be harmonized with Whitehead's creative ontology, and leaves ample room for a hopeful

---

1. "But I would say that mimetic desire, even when bad, is intrinsically good, in the sense that far from being merely imitative in a small sense, it's the opening out of oneself." René Girard, "Violence, Difference, Sacrifice: An Interview with René Girard." Interviewed by Rebecca Adams. In *Violence, Difference, Sacrifice:* A Special Issue of *Religion and Literature* 25 no. 2 (Summer 1993), ed. Rebecca Adams, 11-33. Reprinted in *René Girard: Prophet of Envy,* ed. Cynthia Haven, 51-72. (New York: Bloomsbury Academic, 2020).

2. René Girard, *Evolution and Conversion.* (London: Bloomsbury Revelations), 56.

3. John Milbank, *Theology and Social Theory,* 397–98; "Stories of Sacrifice," *Contagion: Journal of Violence, Mimesis, and Culture* 2 (1995): 75–102, https://doi-org.dtl.idm.oclc.org/10.1353/ctn.1995.0003.

4. Girard said in his 1993 interview with Rebecca Adams that many have misinterpreted his views, "notably John Milbank." Girard, "Violence, Difference, Sacrifice: An Interview with René Girard," 20.

5. Cynthia Haven explores the difficulty Girard had with speaking about his personal conversion within the academic world. See chapter 7 of Cynthia L. Haven, *Evolution of Desire: A Life of René Girard.* (East Lansing: Michigan State University Press, 2018), 148.

future. Without diminishing Girard's sobering and honest view of human history, I will develop his thoughts concerning the revelation of Christ and creative desire further to give them greater emphasis.

Girard's method of inquiry began with literary criticism. This discipline brings to us an inherent appreciation for narrative intelligibility. However, *narrative* for Girard is more than fantasy. Trevor Merrill notes:

> In contrast to the once-fashionable deconstructive school, for which reality is a text, Girard placed great emphasis on his theory's realism: in his view texts speak about concrete reality and not only or primarily about themselves.[6]

Girard believes that great narratives expose our illusions of independent individualism and unveil the relational structure of reality. His first book, *Deceit, Desire, and the Novel* (1961), argues that what distinguishes great novels from the mediocre is the surprising conclusion in which the protagonists experience a type of conversion by recognizing how desire has bound them to their model/rival.[7] This revelation makes a profound reconciliation between the *self* and the *other* possible. In contrast, mediocre novels maintain the 'romantic lie' of an independent self and so remain blind to the true nature of conflict as well. Thus, Girard's literary insights begin spilling over into other disciplines, such as psychology, sociology, and philosophy.

In his second book, *Violence and the Sacred* (1972), Girard analyzes classical origin myths showing that despite cultural differences,

---

6. James Alison and Wolfgang Palaver, eds., *The Palgrave Handbook of Mimetic Theory and Religion*. (New York: Palgrave Macmillan 2017), 459.

7. René Girard, *Deceit, Desire, and the Novel: Self and Other in Literary Structure*. (Baltimore: Johns Hopkins University Press, 2010).

similar events gave birth to similar stories.[8] Structurally, these myths contain elements of mimetic desire, conflict, and what he identifies as scapegoating violence. One can see a definite shift in focus to anthropology in this work. The book received a positive review by G-H de Radkowski in *Le Monde*, heralding it as an "enormous intellectual achievement" and "the first truly atheistic theory of religion and of the sacred."[9] In this context, Girard's third book, *Things Hidden since the Foundation of the World* (1978), came as a surprise. Divided into three sections, it deals with anthropology (no surprise), psychology (no surprise), and the Judeo-Christian Scriptures (surprise!)[10] And so, with this book, Girard enters the theological domain from an anthropological perspective.

The strength of Girard's theological contribution lies in this anthropological approach. However, the theological contribution made by mimetic theory can be limited if it is not contextualized within a creation or cosmological theology. This present work aims to provide a larger context and a trajectory to the Girardian narrative. Both Girard and Whitehead recognize a common weakness among many philosophies in the tendency to become entangled in theory and removed from experience. Mimetic theory provides process philosophy with a more grounded historical narrative, in which its concepts can find concrete application. In turn, process philosophy provides mimetic theory with cosmological context and ontological depth.

---

8. René Girard, *Violence and the Sacred.* (London: Bloomsbury Academic, 2017).

9. Chris Fleming, *René Girard: Violence and Mimesis.* (Cambridge: Polity Press, 2004), 111.

10. René Girard, *Things Hidden since the Foundation of the World.* (London: Bloomsbury Academic, 2016).

Alfred North Whitehead

Whitehead's ideas are an adventurous quest into the nature of reality and the structure of possibility. Whitehead's universe is a living organism, made of intertwining processes—a flux of pulsating, rhythmic, and meaningful events. He shows us how contrasts seek harmony, and in the process, produce tension that fuels a creative advance. These are not mere mechanistic movements—they are more like organisms. For him, processes have an internal dimension that includes all the richness of feeling, motivation, and meaning. To convey this depth of what he means by process, Whitehead uses the word *experience* in a new way to denote a single and most fundamental ontological category.

We can't be disconnected observers with this view of reality. Human experience is not an exception in an otherwise mindless universe; rather, it is an exemplification of, and gives us insight into, the structure and workings of our universe. Whitehead sees his conceptual framework as a "system of general ideas in terms of which every element of our experience can be interpreted."[11] He also recognizes a collective direction to events: "The teleology of the Universe is directed to the production of Beauty."[12] Process philosophy concerns itself not only with explanation but also with appreciation. Reality appeals to our sense of value and worth. Our cosmos is ordered in such a way as to make the actualization of value possible. This value derives from the fact that God's valuation of possibilities is oriented toward truth, beauty, and goodness.

There are many nuanced ways of reading Whitehead. One of his terms, *atomism*, has led to significant differences in interpreting

---

11. Alfred N. Whitehead, *Process and Reality*. Gifford Lectures Delivered in the University of Edinburgh During the Session 1927-28. (New York: Free Press. Kindle Edition), 3.

12. Alfred N. Whitehead, *Adventures of ideas*. (New York: Free Press, 2010), 265.

him, altering the meaning of his philosophy. What did he mean by this term? Many have interpreted Whitehead's atomism, and consequently his concept of an *actual entity*, to refer to very small particles. However, several scholars have opposed this view. Wallack, for instance, describes such an interpretation as reducing Whitehead's philosophy to "a colorful and poetic atomism created for our literary delight." [13] Auxier and Herstein also argue for a more careful reading of Whitehead. They interpret Whitehead's *actual entity/occasion* as both a unit of existence and an explanatory tool:

> . . .we really must stress that Whitehead's concept of the "actual entity" is not a bit of physical existence. It is a conceptual tool that helps the inquirer arrest temporal passage and the flux of the physical universe.[14]

This interpretation of Whitehead is of particular relevance in chapter four where I begin analyzing mimetic processes using this perspective. As will become clear, I interpret *atom* to refer to a unit of value and *epoch* to refer to a unit of time.

Intertwining Narratives

Whitehead and Girard's ideas have inspired many in diverse disciplines. The areas of overlap most relevant for this project are psychology, anthropology, philosophy of religion, and theology. Underlying all these areas of inquiry is Whitehead's understanding

---

13. Wallack, F. Bradford, *The Epochal Nature of Process in Whitehead's Metaphysics*. (Albany: State University of New York Press, 1980), 28, 29.

14. Randall E. Auxier and L. Gary Herstein, *Quantum of Explanation: Whitehead's Radical Empiricism*. (Abingdon, UK: Routledge), 7.

of the nature of reality, his metaphysics. This metaphysical schema provides us with the most creative possibilities for new meaning as we harmonize it with Girard's understanding of the processes that made us human. Whitehead's metaphysics can be further categorized as ontology and cosmology. Ontology considers the nature of reality, including the relationship between mind and matter and between possibility and actuality—what sounds like a standard definition of ontology. However, when we realize that reality refers to something very different within a process approach than in a typical substance approach, the meaning completely changes. Reality refers more to an ontology of becoming than being, for reality is not made of things but processes. This open ontology aims not at certainty but enriched experience. Based on these ontological assumptions, cosmology considers the origins, development, and future of our universe.

Whitehead's ontological claims directly affect Girard's claims regarding the processes that made us human. Mimetic theory can be understood as a series of nested and overlapping processes. Human imitative capacities form the base process on which to build the process of mimetic desire, which is then nested in a more complex relational matrix that births, what Girard describes as the scapegoating process, which then becomes the basis for ritual and religion, and so on. Whitehead's cosmology is inseparable from his ontological principles and seeks to understand the progression and trajectory of processes. As such, his cosmology offers a unique process perspective of Girard's anthropological theory of how humanity, religion, and culture developed and where they may be heading.

Girard and Whitehead are both empirical thinkers—passionate about getting to the actual events that explain our ideas, rather than getting lost in abstract theories. Their respective structures of thought are logically coherent, for the most part.[15] Their ideas also display a narrative intelligibility. The method by which I will bring their thoughts together should inherently include the empirical and logically coherent qualities. However, narrative intelligibility will be the primary method of harmonization. I aim to show that the various claims made by Girard and Whitehead enrich each other in a combined and enlarged narrative.

Mimetic theory naturally lends itself to a narrative progression, starting with the events that made us human, continuing with the evolution of culture and religion, followed by the textual developments in both origin myths and biblical scriptures, and finding a crescendo in the story of Jesus. Although process philosophy does not have such an obvious plot, on an ontological level, Whitehead unveils the narrative capacity in all reality, and on a cosmological level it unites the micro stories and provides a trajectory to the narrative.

Process and *narrative* can be considered equivalent when referring to a structured series of events. Both concepts speak of a pattern of events that unfolds organically. From a substantialist perspective, processes are meaningless mechanical movements, but from the process philosophical perspective, processes have meaning, internal relationships, and teleological aims. Process, in this context, is therefore closely aligned to what is meant by narrative. Whitehead also applies these philosophical insights when he speculates about the origins and history of culture and religion.

In combining these two systems of thought, Whitehead's metaphysics provides both a cosmology and an ontology, complementing mimetic theory. Girard's ideas mainly concern anthropology, but

---

15. Their ideas have been subject to extensive critical scholarship that have highlighted inconsistencies and proposed refinements. Yet, the central ideas have retained their integrity.

include some ontological observations. Within an enlarged story, Whiteheadian cosmology provides a larger context by which the trajectory of the combined narrative becomes clearer. Conversely, the Girardian anthropological narrative provides an opportunity for a concrete application of process concepts, thereby illustrating them in actual human history. In general, Girard enriches Whitehead through exemplification and Whitehead enriches Girard through an expansion of the overall narrative and deeper ontological insights into the processes. New opportunities for either harmony or conflict will emerge through new contrasts between the two discourses as well. As we navigate these potential conflicts, we embark on an adventure that can steer us to a beautiful new space: a larger and more useful meaning-making framework.

Some Girardian and Whiteheadian concepts have direct correlations and fit naturally into an ontological category. By ontological category, I mean that it is within the nature of reality for processes to have repeatable patterns. For instance, the *process* concepts of *prehension* and *appetition*[16] correlate with the concept of *mimetic desire*.[17] On a larger narrative scale, Whitehead's idea that history has a general direction, moving from force to persuasion, might complement Girard's idea that sacrificial violence undergoes a radical critique, culminating in the death of Christ which opens a new non-violent possibility of being human. But Whitehead and Girard also may disagree, especially about the evolution of religion and civilization. For Whitehead, the pursuit of beauty and peace fundamentally grounds the development of both religion and civilization. In contrast, Girard sees scapegoating violence as the origin and

---

16. Defined in Chapter 2.
17. Defined in Chapter 3.

generative event behind religion and culture. These ideas so fundamentally inform their respective narratives that we may wonder if their potential incompatibility will greatly reduce the value of bringing the narratives together.

However, we should be able to overcome these potential obstacles and create what Whitehead calls, a novel complex harmony, greatly enriching the theological contributions made by each framework. Open and relational theology is a category that explores the non-deterministic nature of reality (openness) and the extent to which God is involved in temporal reality. Process philosophy explicitly supports open and relational theological views.[18] Mimetic theory, in contrast, does not make many explicit statements about God. Rather, as its anthropological narrative unfolds, it is through the radical transformation of meaning that the true nature of God is implied. Are open and relational ideas implicitly present in mimetic theory? We'll explore this question. I aim to make these implied meanings more explicit.

Whitehead passed away before Girard developed his ideas but as we'll see, many of his questions anticipated Girard's ideas. We know Girard was at least aware of Whitehead, for in an article examining Girard's place amongst philosophers, the author notes that Girard once quoted Whitehead.[19] The book Girard quoted from was, unsurprisingly, *Religion in the Making*.[20] Girard writes: 'In 1926, A. N. Whitehead deplored our situation, in which 'Christianity lacks a

---

18. Open and relational theologians might not support all the tenets of process philosophy. However, the openness and relational nature of reality are key principles for process philosophy and as such it explicitly supports open and relational theological views.

19. Guy Vanheeswijck, "The Place of René Girard in Contemporary Philosophy." Contagion: Journal of Violence, Mimesis, and Culture 10, (2003): 95-110. doi:10.1353/ctn.2003.0004.

20. Alfred N. Whitehead, *Religion in the Making: Lowell Lectures, 1926.* (Cambridge: Cambridge University Press, 2011).

clear-cut separation from the crude fancies of the older tribal religions.'"[21] So Girard had at least a rudimentary acquaintance with Whitehead's thought.

Any introduction to either Girard or Whitehead could easily fill a book, as scholars of these figures know. Indeed, many excellent resources do just that. So, instead of providing comprehensive overviews of their ideas, I will adopt a strategy stressing the aim of overall narrative intelligibility mentioned before. The next two chapters are written in a narrative style, introducing the respective theories of Whitehead and Girard. These stories will serve as background paintings, providing the outlines of a plot within which the progression of meaning will find context. Detailed analysis commences in chapter four. This narrative style might differ from that commonly used in academic works, but that is the function of backgrounds—they need to be less technically focused to emphasize the details to come.

---

21. René Girard, *Je Vois Satan Tomber Comme L'éclair*. (Paris: Grasset, 2016), 9.

2

Becoming—A Cosmic Story

If you have read any philosophy, you might have come to the same
conclusion as Whitehead, namely, that some of these wild speculations are so abstract that their connection to reality is difficult to
discern. Yet, in many cases, these abstract fantasies pretend to represent reality. Whitehead laments:

> Philosophical thought has made for itself difficulties by deal-
> ing exclusively in very abstract notions … The result is that
> philosophical discussion is enmeshed in the fallacy of 'mis-
> placed concreteness.'[1]

The "fallacy of misplaced concreteness" refers to the erro-
neous way we treat abstractions as concrete realities. In contrast,
Whitehead is determined "to base philosophical thought upon the
most concrete elements in our experience." As ideas develop, abstraction and interpretation become inevitable. But one can avoid
the fallacy of misplaced concreteness by starting the journey with a

---

1. Whitehead, *Process and Reality*, 18.

careful observation of actual experience, developing the necessary interpretations and finally returning to experience to test the validity of these ideas.

The more abstract our ideas, the more dependent they become on interpretation. Interpretation makes both novelty and error possible. But failure to recognize our abstractions as interpretations can have the unfortunate effect of dogmatic certainty. Whitehead again warns us: "Philosophy has been afflicted by the dogmatic fallacy, which is the belief that the principles of its working hypotheses are clear, obvious, and irreformable."[2] This is especially significant for his ontological claims, as they are not rigidly set in dogmatic certainty.[3] Rather, he sees philosophical inquiry as "adventures" that are meant to intensify our experience. Consequently, for him an ideal practice of philosophy takes on a very different form: "Philosophy begins in wonder. And, at the end, when philosophic thought has done its best, the wonder remains. "[4]

I believe this is a profound invitation for everyone to enter into the wonder of existence, for the intelligibility of our universe is not hidden in a fanciful abstract theory. Instead, we find the key that unlocks these wonders in the immediacy of our experience. Whitehead shows great confidence in appealing to our intuition.[5] Experience has a depth of meaning accessible to anyone who approaches it with the awe and careful observation it deserves. Process philosophy has an inherent reverence to it, for it respects the uniqueness, creativity, and value of every element of existence. For in every fragment of

---

2. Whitehead, Adventures of Ideas, 223.

3. "Metaphysical categories are not dogmatic statements of the obvious; they are tentative formulations of the ultimate generalities." Whitehead, *Process and Reality*, 8.

4. Alfred. N. Whitehead, *Modes of Thought*. (New York: Free Press, 2010), 168.

5. "The sole appeal is to intuition." Whitehead, *Process and Reality*, 21.

existence, including yourself, the universal logic of what's actual and what's possible finds a unique expression.

This vision of reality sees our universe as a unifying verse. The detail does not diminish the wonder of the enormity of this living cosmos, but exemplifies it. Every process is art in motion, giving a unique perspective of the whole. Consequently, every part within this cosmic body relates to every other part and contains a rich history of interaction. From the tapestry of actuality and its history of intertwinement, we glean insights into the structure of possibility steering its progress.

This approach shapes Whitehead's methods and tools of inquiry. If reality consists of interwoven structured events rather than *things*, then we have as our objects of inquiry movements rather than static substances. We should therefore adjust our methods and tools for the task. We find in Whitehead's *Process and Reality* as much a development of the methods of inquiry as the development of metaphysical concepts. Whitehead prepares us: "the unity of treatment is to be looked for in the gradual development of the schema, in meaning and in relevance, and not in the successive treatment of particular topics."[6] We can therefore say that Whitehead's methodology is radically empirical and has a narrative intelligibility about it. His metaphysical framework does not compete with scientific knowledge but accommodates it and broadens our knowledge of our world and ourselves.

There is another way of viewing this cosmos, a perspective that does not recognize the internal and meaningful connections that form the whole. Instead, from this perspective the universe is imagined as consisting of countless, tiny, dead things which occasionally

---

6. Whitehead, *Process and Reality*, xii.

clump together to make bigger dead things. These entities move according to predetermined paths set by external laws. They have no interior freedom and mean nothing to themselves or to one another.

In this view, the instances where life cannot be ignored are simply treated as highly exceptional accidents. Human consciousness is viewed as such an unnatural accident, it's considered to be either a different type of substance altogether, or an anomaly not worth our attention. This alternative perspective values certainty above beauty and therefore limits the questions it asks to those that can be answered by counting and measuring.

The Process Approach

We can take two approaches when considering the nature of reality, what exists, and how to understand it. We can begin with substances and explain all activity as actions taken by these substances (commonly called a "substance view"), or we can begin with activity and explain all substances as the result of dynamic processes (also known as a "process view"). Process philosophy prioritizes activity over substance and change over persistence. This doesn't mean that process thought denies the existence of substances, but rather that substances are but one type of product of process, and the being or essence of a substance is in its becoming. Descartes defines a substance as: "an existent thing which requires nothing other than itself to exist."[7] Process philosophy disagrees with this substantialist view and redefines a substance as the coming together of the whole into a microscopic perspective—a distillation of all relationships. An existent thing requires everything to exist for it is a perspective

---

7. Principles of Philosophy, I.51.

of its world. In a world where everything is intertwined, every part implicates the whole.

What is most real is the living movement—process. For instance, when seeing a flower, one sees more than a form consisting of smaller particles. The flower embodies a history of processes that made it what it now appears to be. The flower tells a story of co-creative relationships between plants and soil, plants and bacteria, and plants and insects. In fact, each of the particles in this flower has a story that has shaped it and positioned it in the unique expression of this flower. These creative processes are living in the sense that they are animated by an internal responsiveness to possibilities and not simply determined by external laws.

There are other types of events that don't persist in a substantial embodied form, yet are just as real. For example, a tsunami, a conversation, and a symphonic performance all have real existence.

A process can be defined as a coordinated movement of events, a structured series of changes that reaches into both the past and the future by its very nature. A process may consist of many sub-processes. The blooming of a flower has both a history and a future entangled in one overarching process. As such, a process incorporates both efficient causality (the influence of the past) and teleological objectives (the influence of the future/possibilities) in a complex interconnected activity. In the substantialist view, separate things only exist in this moment and relate to other things externally. In contrast, the process view recognizes the essential connection between the past and the future and the complexity of internal relationships that shape reality.

Category of the Ultimate

A categorical schema within metaphysics refers to the way we organize our thoughts about reality. Remember, according to Whitehead, we should begin this narrative journey with the least abstract and most concrete elements of experience. To do this, one has to identify these concrete elements of experience as clearly as possible and the context/whole in which they occur. Consequently, he begins his inquiry with one of the oldest metaphysical questions: are we dealing with one reality or a multiplicity? Is the whole one or many? And he famously answers: "the many become one and are increased by one." The category of the Ultimate has to do with the most general characteristics of reality: the many and the one and the creative nature of their interaction. It is the first category in which the subsequent categories of *existence, explanation,* and *obligation* find their context and meaning.

To make Whitehead's ideas more accessible, I imagine the richness of this whole as follows: We experience reality as both one continual flow and as a multiplicity of events intertwined. When we approach reality in all its complexity and wholeness, recognizing the dynamic and interwoven nature of its fabric, then explaining the distinctness of an event, a fact, or a thing, becomes no simple task. For example, a tapestry might depict a scene from nature in which specific elements, such as trees, rivers, animals, and people can be identified. Yet, on closer inspection, these distinct elements are part of threads extending into the rest of the tapestry. These distinct elements don't have independent existence. If we were to explain them, we would have to refer to the world in which they find themselves. Although distinct, they are intertwined. The tapestry example illustrates the point that distinct elements in our experience have extensions beyond what seems like obvious boundaries. But of course, the example is also oversimplified. Reality remains more complex. We could make the illustration more adequate by imagining a multi-dimensional, living tapestry that creates itself, with threads drawing values from the past in one direction and possibilities from the future in another direction. Where the threads meet, unique patterns and values form. All the unique processes have one quality in common—creativity. Whitehead writes:

> 'Creativity' is the universal of universals characterizing ultimate matter of fact. It is that ultimate principle by which the many, which are the* universe disjunctively, become the one actual occasion, which is the universe conjunctively. It lies in the nature of things that the many enter into complex unity.
>
> 'Creativity' is the principle of novelty. An actual occasion is a novel entity diverse from any entity in the' many' which it unifies. Thus 'creativity' introduces novelty into the content of the many, which are the universe disjunctively. The 'creative advance' is the application of this ultimate principle of creativity to each novel situation which it originates.[8]

The *universe disjunctively*, in regard to our illustration, refers to the many unique and distinct patterns that this living tapestry has already formed. The *universe conjunctively* is the one pattern being formed as the many contribute their unique values to a single new instance of reality that exemplifies the whole.

Whitehead describes *creativity* as the process by which the many diverse and contrasting aspects of the universe are harmonized into a novel and new unity. Creativity best identifies the most universal characteristic present in every actual occasion. The many occasions come together into a unique new unity, and this one new occasion enlarges the universe, the whole. While the whole enables

---

8. Whitehead, *Process and Reality*, 21.

19

novel fragments, each fragment enables a new whole. Expanding Whitehead's thought theologically, creativity can be seen as an oscillating movement between the many and the one, a pulsating incarnational rhythm in which the 'Logos' finds flesh moment by moment, instance upon instance.[9]

Significantly, this movement has a trajectory. The novelty produced by creativity is not simply a chaotic variety; instead, it is a creative *advance*. In philosophy, explaining something based on its movement toward a purpose is called teleology. In recognizing the teleological trajectory of this creative advance, the concept of God becomes most relevant. Whitehead does not invoke God as an explanation for a system of thought that cannot stand by itself. Rather, within his metaphysical schema, God is the most appropriate name for the lure toward beauty. Our world awakens in us more than a desire to measure and count (scientific knowledge); it awakes an appreciation for the value of relationship and the meaning of love. Even if nature contains within itself all the explanatory features necessary to make its existence intelligible, we must acknowledge a dimension of experience beyond the order of explanation, only accessible through the order of appreciation. Seen this way, God is not so much the explanation for our world as the inspiration for our enjoyment of it.[10]

Whitehead's philosophical approach runs into a few challenges because it doesn't artificially avoid the complexity of reality. We

---

9. The Gospel of John has a similar view of God, envisioning God as Logos—a logic and a word that seeks material existence. See John 1.

10. "The service it [process theology] sees the divine as rendering to human understanding does not lie in the order of causal explanation but rather in the order of evaluative appreciation—in enabling us to apprehend more correctly and realistically the grounds and indications of the fact that the world's arrangements can have worth and value." Nicholas Rescher, *Process Metaphysics: An Introduction to Process Philosophy*. (Albany: State University of New York Press, 1996), 161.

are dealing with a living organism, interconnected, and constantly evolving. I identify three complexities inherent in this approach, namely, that (1) reality constantly changes, (2) everything is entangled, and (3) these relationships are patterned according to a structure of possibility inherent in our cosmos.

Category of Existence

To gain insight into the nature of reality, one needs to identify the distinct elements that need explanation. Whitehead identifies eight categories of existence. All eight categories are patterns of process that form part of the most fundamental pattern, what he calls the *actual entity*. Whitehead notes: "in the becoming of an actual entity, novel prehensions, nexus, subjective forms, propositions, multiplicities, and contrasts, also become; but there are no novel eternal objects."[11] He also draws attention to the fact that "Among these eight categories of existence, actual entities and eternal objects stand out with a certain extreme finality."[12] Eternal objects refer to nontemporal possibilities—they are not subject to change. Put more simply: reality consists of what is actual and what is possible. We'll explore each of these categories as and when they become relevant to our narrative.

Basic Unit of Meaning

We have already established that reality constantly changes, processes are intertwined, and each completed process adds something novel to the whole. If everything is interconnected, how does one divide reality into portions for further study? The most meaningful

---

11. Whitehead, *Process and Reality*, 22
12. Ibid.

way to divide these processes, according to Whitehead, is to identify a portion that produces a definite fact or value: "the final problem is to conceive a complete fact. We can only form such a conception in terms of fundamental notions concerning the nature of reality."[13]

Consequently, Whitehead develops a conceptual tool, a basic unit of explanation, by which we can identify a meaningful slice of reality—what he calls a "complete fact," a pulse of realized value. We can then limit the transformative movements of this process to an indivisible duration, or *epoch,* in his terminology. Epoch, in this context, means to pause or arrest. For the sake of explanation, we pause a unit of process together with its world and treat it as an indivisible whole—what Whitehead calls an *atom.* He uses *atom* in the original Greek sense of the word to denote wholeness or indivisibility. So, for Whitehead, the term *epoch* serves as a unit of time, and *atom* serves as a unit of value within his metaphysical schema. This unit is indivisible not because of its simplicity or singleness but because of its togetherness, its unity of meaning. Within this whole, complexity remains: "atomism does not exclude complexity and universal relativity. Each atom is a system of all things."[14]

One could compare this unit, or atom, to a chapter in a story or a scene within a movie. The scene only makes sense within the context of the whole movie, yet by introducing some virtual boundaries, one can replay it as many times as necessary to explore its meaning. In the real world, we can't pause the flow of events or record them in the fullness of their actuality. So, Whitehead develops a philosophical tool by which he attempts to come as close as possible to

---

13. Whitehead, *Adventures of ideas*, 158.
14. Whitehead, *Process and Reality*, 35.

arresting the flux. We overcome the first obstacle—that of constant change—by pausing a unit of process.

This unit of explanation serves as an abstract representation of a concrete slice of reality.[15] As such it belongs to both the category of existence and the category of explanation. With this method, Whitehead captures the most fundamental ontological category. Ontology, in philosophy, has to do with an explanation of the most fundamental nature of things. He reminds us that the "explanatory purpose of philosophy is often misunderstood. Its business is to explain the emergence of the more abstract things from the more concrete things."[16] However, the purpose of explanation is not to arrive at a complete and final understanding; instead, he says explanation serves as "an adventure in the clarification of thought."[17]

Furthermore, this clarification of thought should help us better interpret experience and so enrich it.[18] Whitehead's method of philosophical inquiry has a double movement, starting with careful observation of experience, then moving toward the more abstract patterns and structures of possibility to gain universal insights, and finally returning to experience to evaluate if these insights can be verified. He terms these basic units of explanation "actual entities":

---

15. Auxier and Herstein shows that the *actual entity* belongs to both the order of existence and the order of explanation. "Yet, we really must stress that Whitehead's concept of the 'actual entity' is not a bit of physical existence. It is a conceptual tool that helps the inquirer arrest temporal passage and the flux of the physical universe. The concept of the actual entity is the most important in a collection of logical tools doing this work of holding the object of inquiry in stasis while it is analyzed. That "holding" cannot be achieved without some distortion entering the picture, but nothing will yield to analysis without some means of rendering it an object of study." See Auxier, *Quantum of Explanation*, 7.

16. Whitehead, *Process and Reality*, 20.

17. Ibid., 9.

18. Ibid., 3.

'Actual entities'—also termed 'actual occasions'—are the final real things of which the world is made up. There is no going behind actual entities to find anything more real. They differ among themselves: God is an actual entity, and so is the most trivial puff of existence in far-off empty space. But, though there are gradations of importance, and diversities of function, yet in the principles which actuality exemplifies all are on the same level. The final facts are, all alike, actual entities; and these actual entities are drops of experience, complex and interdependent.[19]

The actual entity allows us to identify and speak of discrete processes within the entangled flux that is our universe. As such Whitehead's concept of actual entity is relevant to the mimetic processes we will explore in the next chapter. The actual entity is a way of understanding the relation between the many fragments, the one, and the whole—the facts within the inexhaustible mystery. Whitehead specifies two descriptions that are required for an actual entity:

(a) one which is analytical of its potentiality for 'objectification' in the becoming of other actual entities, and (b) another which is analytical of the process which constitutes its own becoming. The term 'objectification' refers to the particular mode in which the potentiality of one actual entity is realized in another actual entity. That how an actual entity becomes constitutes what that actual entity is; so that the two descriptions of an actual entity are not independent. Its

---

19. Ibid., 18.

'being' is constituted by its 'becoming.' This is the 'principle of process.'[20]

These two descriptions are also referred to as *genetic* and *coordinate* perspectives. In this context, "genetic" derives from the Greek word "genesis," which means origin or mode of production. Genetic analysis, therefore, refers to the study of the origins, development, and unfolding of processes. It's an examination of how something comes to be, how it evolves, and how it relates to other entities or processes.

Coordinate analysis, on the other hand, focuses on the value, the fact, or the outcome of the process and how that outcome becomes a potential to be realized in other actual entities. The concept of *prehension* helps us with both these descriptive perspectives.

Prehensions

The word *relationship* can be understood in a variety of ways. Whitehead clarifies what he means by relationship and uses the term *prehension* to convey this enriched meaning.[21] A prehension, for Whitehead, is a relationship that has an internal and creative dimension to it. These relationships don't only exist *between* entities, but are *formative* of entities.[22] Entities feel the influences of others and these feelings become aspects of their own existence.

For example, an apple is the product of innumerable relational movements: The relationships between bacteria and soil, the soil and the apple tree, the tree and the weather, every chemical transformation within the tree, and so on. The apple doesn't just have

---

20. Ibid., 23.

21. Ibid., 20, 219.

22. "Actual entities involve each other by reason of their prehensions of each other." Ibid., 20.

relationships; it is itself constituted of these creative movements. We can use prehensions (internal and creative dimensions of the relationship) to describe the apple genetically: that is, as processes that produced the apple; and coordinately, that is, as the final outcome of these processes, which would be an actual apple having potential value to other entities.

The second obstacle we identified earlier to understanding reality from this process perspective is the complexity of interconnected relationships. Whitehead helps us overcome this complexity by his concept of prehensions. We said that we can pause the flow of experience for the sake of examining it, like examining a scene in a movie. Having paused an actual occasion, we can now analyze it from an inexhaustible series of perspectives. Each perspective focuses on a particular relationship or prehension.

We can't aim to analyze all the prehensions in a given situation, for that would be impossible. Whitehead doesn't attempt to create comprehensive knowledge but instead useful knowledge, relevant to the inquiry. He notes that prehensions "express the most concrete mode of analysis applicable to every grade of individual actuality"[23] and that each "actual entity is 'divisible' in an indefinite number of ways, and each way of 'division' yields its definite quota of prehensions."[24] We established earlier that an actual occasion is an indivisible unit. So, what does Whitehead mean when he says prehensions divide the actual entity? These are logical divisions for the sake of analysis.

Let's develop the movie scene metaphor further. To capture a 360-degree video involves a unique set of challenges and

---

23. Ibid., 19.
24. Ibid.

considerations compared to traditional video recording. It requires multiple cameras and specialized equipment configured to capture all angles. After capturing the scene, more complex processes follow. The footage from each camera must be "stitched" together in post-production to create a seamless 360-degree view. What we now have is a means by which to examine the scene from all angles. Our means of capturing and analyzing the event from different angles does not actually divide the scene/event. The scene itself remains a complex whole. But we now have a method of analyzing the scene from many angles. In this same way, prehensions logically divide actual entities.

Every fragment in the whole of reality is an actualization of what is possible within this whole; we have a harmonization of the whole into a microscopic perspective. The fragment would not be what it is without the whole, and the whole would not be what it is without the fragment. Each fragment feels (or prehends) the influence of all the other fragments and interprets those influences in such a way that it uniquely shapes (through subjective form) the feeling into an aspect of the fragment. Within this metaphysical schema, God serves as the ultimate whole that envelops all possibility, all actuality, and the history of their complex interactions.

Thus, the whole universe is an available resource to the process in which a new occasion becomes actual. Whitehead writes: "Accordingly the full universe, disclosed for every variety of experience, is a universe in which every detail enters into its proper relationship with the immediate occasion."[25] Moreover, the universe does not consist of actualities alone; the universe is also home to a structure of possibility, a treasure trove of potential novelty. In this

---

25. Whitehead, *Science and the Modern World*, 25.

process of actualization, all the facts/actualities enter into their relevant relationship with the immediate occasion, but only a selection of possibilities are actualized.

Some possibilities are felt to be unnecessary or incompatible with the new experience and Whitehead terms these *negative prehensions*.[26] Consequently, the actual entity eliminates these from feeling. Nevertheless, by their very absence they contribute something unique to the new occasion. Whitehead distinguishes between prehensions that interpret the data of other actual entities—which he calls *physical prehensions*—and prehensions that interpret possibilities into novel harmonies—what he calls *conceptual prehensions*.[27] Whitehead gives the name *appetition* to the positive feeling of possibilities. Put more simply: desire is how an entity feels the future. Positive prehensions are unconscious apprehensions of the aspects of other fragments of the whole and possibilities as they are brought into a new harmony and internal unity. This harmony represents a new intensity and diversity of experience.

This unification has another dimension as well. Actual occasions can give endurance to identities that span multiple occasions. For example, a season within the lifespan of a tree can be abstracted as an actual occasion. However, this season is part of a larger story. The similarity of the pattern of unification from instance to instance preserves identity. Prehensions not only take what's 'there' and bring it into relationship with the 'here' but also absorb what's of value from the previous instance of existence to unite it with what is of

---

26. That there are two species of prehensions: (a) 'positive prehensions' which are termed 'feelings,' and (b) 'negative prehensions' which are said to 'eliminate from feeling.' Whitehead, *Process and Reality*, 23.

27. Ibid., 23.

possible value in the future. An actual entity is an instance in which all the resources of this universe, everything out there, everything past, and everything desirable in the future, are harmonized into a unique value that can contribute meaning to the next instance of existence. Prehensions are both the process and the concrete facts of relatedness.[28]

Whitehead, therefore, directly contradicts Aristotle's claim that a substance cannot be present in another substance. Whitehead regards this relational presence as a critical concept within process philosophy: "If we allow for degrees of relevance, and for negligible relevance, we must say that every actual entity is present in every other actual entity. The philosophy of organism is mainly devoted to the task of making clear the notion of 'being present in another entity.'"[29] Some relationships are stronger and more relevant than others, yet no matter how weak, every part relates to every other part. Nothing exists outside of relationship. For Whitehead, the very constitution of reality is a relational mesh that connects every actuality with all other actualities:

The misconception which has haunted philosophic literature throughout the centuries is the notion of 'independent existence'. There is no such mode of existence; every entity is only to be understood in terms of the way in which it is interwoven with the rest of the Universe.[30]

---

28. "Each process of appropriation of a particular element is termed a prehension." Whitehead, *Process and Reality*, 219.

29. Ibid., 50.

30. Whitehead, Alfred. N. *Essays in Science and Philosophy: Personal; Philosophy; Education; Science.* (New York: Philosophical Library, 1947), 64.

Process philosophy introduces a revolutionary, different philosophical approach to that common in Western substance metaphysics—a transformation from a belief in substances unaffected by relationship, to an understanding that relationship gives substance to everything. It's important to emphasize that for Whitehead, these relationships are not only external but internal. A similar revolutionary understanding emerged within Quantum Physics. In a conversation with Einstein, Heisenberg speaks of his experience when discovering this interior world: "I had the feeling that, through the surface of atomic phenomena, I was looking at a strangely beautiful interior."[31] Instead of a world of substances that relate externally to other substances, in process thought we have an internally relational reality.

As we will see more clearly later, we can find a relational view of reality in mimetic theory as well. In his masterwork, *Things Hidden Since the Foundation of the World,* Girard's conversation with Guy Lefort and psychologist Jean-Michel Oughourlian gives rise to the newly-coined expression "interdividual psychology." With this concept, Girard conveyed that they wanted to express their "conviction that the monadic subject doesn't exist, that the self is formed only in relations with the other."[32]

A New Ontology

Whitehead's vision of a singular ontological type of existence, the actual occasion, is a fundamental move away from substance dualism and gives process philosophy a significant conceptual advantage.

---

31. Werner Heisenberg. *Physics and Beyond.* (London: Allen & Unwin, 1981), 58-69.

32. Although Girard doesn't use this particular term much in all of his work outside *Things Hidden*, its basic meaning is always present in his work. See Jean-Michel Oughourlian, *The Mimetic Brain, Studies in Violence, Mimesis, & Culture,* (Michigan State University Press, 2016), 33.

Whitehead compares and contrasts his ontology with Descartes and Locke:

> With the purpose of obtaining a one-substance cosmology, 'prehensions' are a generalization from Descartes' mental 'cogitations,' and from Locke's 'ideas,' to express the most concrete mode of analysis applicable to every grade of individual actuality. Descartes and Locke maintained a two-substance ontology—Descartes explicitly, Locke by implication.[33]

Descartes and Locke believe the world is composed of two types of things—mind and matter. But for Whitehead, all that exists is made of one type of thing, rather than two. To convey the relational complexity and internal unity of any actual entity, Whitehead uses the word *experience* in a new way, as a concept that combines both physical and subjective aspects of reality. What Whitehead is calling an actual entity is a center of experience. Through its prehensions, he says the occasion or actual entity feels the influence of its world and harmonizes those influences into an internal unity. We will explore what this means.

We best understand the meaning of experience in the context of human experience. Experiences can be identified individually—each is an actual occasion. An experience might be as simple as the enjoyment of a meal. Alternatively, I may expand my awareness and consider my experience of the day, which includes the experience of the meal but produces a larger unity of feeling. Again, I could enlarge my awareness and consider the meaning of my life as a whole—all

---

33. Whitehead, *Process and Reality*, 19.

experiences, including my anticipation of the future. The unity of feeling, this center of experience, doesn't have any particular size or duration. Its time is created by its own process and is indivisible—a unit of time measured by the unity of feeling. However trivial the experience of a meal may seem, it also includes, unconsciously, the history that brought me to this particular occasion of experience. And however profound the largest awareness of what and who I am might be, it is a unification of feelings to which the most trivial experiences of my life have also contributed some value.

For Whitehead, an actual occasion always includes other occasions in its constitution. He terms the values produced by this togetherness, *nexus*.[34] If we consider humans to be part of the natural world, then the complexity of human experience should have simple elements in common with less complex entities, as Whitehead so aptly states. He shows what is at stake with his thesis:

> Any doctrine which refuses to place human experience outside nature, must find in descriptions of human experience factors which also enter into the descriptions of less specialized natural occurrences. If there be no such factors, the doctrine of human experience as a fact within nature is mere bluff. … We should either admit dualism, … or we should point out the identical elements connecting human experience with physical science.[35]

Human experience can be understood as a complex and intensified occasion, exemplifying what happens on every level of existence.

---

34. Ibid., 20.

35. Whitehead, *Adventures of ideas*, 185.

Every process is an integrated happening that feels the influence of its world and is constituted, to a larger or lesser degree, by all the other actual occasions. Every object (one form of process) has a history and a possible future. Substance dualism, on the other hand, has traditionally separated mind from matter, which allows it to deal with physical objects without considering any internal relational, or historic, complexities. However, the substance approach creates a plethora of problems: substantialism believes that entities can exist in a moment of time with no inner dimension of becoming. It separates the entity from the reality of time, as Whitehead notes: "the lapse of time is an accident, rather than of the essence of the material … The material is equally itself at an instance of time."[36] From this substantialist perspective, objects have to be mindless and exist with no necessary connection to their past. This gives us an entity with no experience, no intrinsic duration or value, something named a "vacuous actuality" by Whitehead. He simply considers vacuous actualities impossible.[37]

In contradiction to substantialism, Whitehead shows that entities exist in the context of the relational experiences that formed them. Our stories, our histories, form an intrinsic part of what we are in this moment. And this is not only true of humans; rather, all entities have both external and internal relations. These experiencing entities are the constituents of reality, or as Whitehead calls them, *drops of experience.*[38] They come in different sizes and complexities. For instance, even the smallest particles known to quantum

---

36. Whitehead, Alfred. N. *Science and the Modern World.* (New York: Open Road Media, 2021), 50.

37. See Whitehead, *Process and Reality*, 167 and Whitehead, Alfred. N. *Modes of Thought.* (New York: Free Press, 2010), 158.

38. Whitehead, *Process and Reality*, 18.

physics have a responsiveness to possibility and as such have a form of subjectivity. Consequently, within process philosophy we need no convoluted explanation for how a different kind of something called "mind" emerges out of mindless material. That problem has been created by substance metaphysics and doesn't plague process thought.

Scientists have found evidence for this inner dimension of experience in non-human entities. The ethologist Donald Griffin shows that different sciences have been pushing the phenomenon of experience further down to include beings and entities beyond the human. Animal ethologists' observations of dolphins, apes, and bees reveal levels of experience.[39] Biologists have made the case for decision-making on the level of prokaryotic cells.[40] Quantum physicists have shown renewed interest in correlating Whiteheadian concepts to quantum processes, including the concept of experience.[41]

Value, Meaning, and Narrative

Having considered the meaning of experience, let's adjust our focus and consider the experience of *meaning*. The historical paths that lead to the actualization of an individual—whether that be a particle, a cell, a human body, or a civilization—reveals a record of creative interpretations and unfolding meaning. Each successive instance experiences the creative interpretation of the previous instance as impressions that are available for its own creative interpretation.

---

39. Donald Griffin, *Animal Minds*. (Chicago: University of Chicago Press. 2013).

40. Julius Adler and Wing-Wai Tse. 1974. "Decision-Making in Bacteria." *Science* 184 (June 21): 1292–1294.

41. "The evolutionary valuation of potentia in quantum mechanics can be correlated phase by phase, and concept by concept, with Whitehead's metaphysical schema, such that the former can be characterized as the fundamental physical exemplification of the latter." (Michael Epperson, *Quantum Mechanics: And the Philosophy of Alfred North Whitehead.* [Fordham University Press, 2019], 10.)

The patterns of intelligibility formed by these processes comprise an accumulation of meaning.[42] For instance, the fossilized rings of a tree stump tell a story. Meaning accumulates in the pattern of its material. The interactions and interdependencies between insects, flowers, and birds speak of a history of co-creativity. We can see how all of reality carries an inherent narrative capacity. Experience, meaning-making, and narrative development are inseparable processes, recorded in the actual material of our world.

Consciousness

Traditional substance metaphysics has a "problem" it tries to solve, namely, how consciousness emerged from matter. Whiteheadian metaphysics turns the question about the emergence of consciousness on its head, for if experience permeates our world, then all the ingredients for conscious experience are already present in the most elementary building blocks of reality. "[C]onsciousness presupposes experience, and not experience consciousness," says Whitehead.[43] The potential for consciousness lies dormant in all material existence in the form of experience. The origins of physical material and consciousness are, therefore, equally mysterious. Instead of asking how mindless material could cause the emergence of consciousness, the question now is focused on the complexity of data synthesis: What are the differences between elementary experience and conscious

---

42. Serpil Oppermann, using Charles Hartshorne concept of Compound Individual, shows how many disciplines in natural sciences now recognize the narrative agency in all material reality. "Hartshorne's insights are also congruent with material ecocriticism, which extends the creativity material agencies further, affirming their expressive dynamics as narrative agency. Emerging in meaningfully articulate forms of becoming, matter is thus interpreted as storied matter encoded with a mesh of meanings, unfolding stories, and narrative trajectories" (Serpil Oppermann, Nature's narrative agencies as compound individuals" *Neohelicon* 44 [2017]: 283–295).

43. Whitehead, *Process and Reality*, 53.

experience? Different grades of consciousness and the boundaries between them become the focus of inquiry.[44]

Robert Mesle finds the emergence of conscious awareness unsurprising, tracing its development: "as these elementary drops of feeling are organized into successively more complex forms, like molecules and cells and animal bodies, central nervous systems and brains, the complexity of those feelings will increase until it crosses a crucial threshold into conscious self-awareness such as you are having right now."[45] The intensification and complexification of desire, symbolic and narrative abilities, and self-awareness is what leads to human consciousness. Chapter five contains a more thorough exploration of this theme.

God

We have alluded before to how Whitehead thinks about God within this metaphysical schema. God, for some, is just the name we invoke when our explanations of reality no longer make sense. In this context, God becomes the reason for what we can't explain intelligently. For others, God is an unnecessary concept. Many process philosophers don't define themselves as theists. In contrast to both these stances, Whitehead refers to God as the very source of the intelligibility of our universe. He believes the primordial nature of God provides the structure of possibility that shapes actuality. He terms this structure of possibility *eternal objects* and so begins to address the third obstacle we identified, namely, the relationship between actuality and possibility. In each process, some of these

---

44. "What needs explaining is not so much how or why consciousness arises at the highest levels of brain function, as why it appears largely absent from lower levels of functioning." Michel Weber and Anderson Weekes, *Process Approaches to Consciousness in Psychology, Neuroscience, and Philosophy of Mind.* (Albany, NY: SUNY Press, 2011), Kindle Location 992).

45. Robert C. Mesle, *Process-Relational Philosophy.* (Templeton Press, 2008), 37.

divinely ordered possibilities are actualized. Consequently, the mind of God finds actual existence. Theologically we can extrapolate this idea and say that nature itself becomes the voice of God—a notion supported by the author of Psalm 19:1-4:

> The heavens declare the glory of God;
>> the skies proclaim the work of his hands.
> Day after day they pour forth speech;
>> night after night they reveal knowledge.
> They have no speech, they use no words;
>> no sound is heard from them.
> Yet their voice goes out into all the earth,
>> their words to the ends of the world.

This process perspective unveils creation as incarnation.[46] The beauty preserved in structures of possibility becomes distilled in temporal and actual drops of experience. These conceptual valuations find actual value in every occasion and so God ontologically saturates our world. This God is not separate but involved with every occasion, influencing every event, yet without control. Yet, in every process of creative advance, we find a stage in which the occasion transcends God—a moment of freedom in which decisions are made, not by God, but by the event itself. Both freedom and genuine evil become possible in this space of creaturely transcendence.

God's relationship to creativity becomes transformed in this process worldview. From a Whiteheadian process perspective, creativity is a relational activity that exemplifies persuasive power and renounces coercive power. Process implies change. Change

---

46. "Each creative act is the universe incarnating itself as one." Whitehead, *Process and Reality*, 245.

can be understood as weak (transformative) or strong (creative). Transformative change refers to a re-arrangement of what is. New patterns emerge out of old patterns of existence. But strong change proves generative, disrupting our world with novelty that can be called truly new. In evaluating Whitehead's concept of creativity, Michel Weber observes:

> Process and Reality's (1929) "creative advance" claims that genuine novelty can only enter the World in a disruptive, bud-like manner. Its point is to secure true becoming, to make the emergence of the unexpected possible within the fabric of the universe. "Process and individuality require each other": change is creation or, better, creativity.[47]

Whitehead therefore qualifies his view of process as entailing a strong generative conception of creativity. He writes: "'[C]reativity,' in the dictionary sense of the verb create, [means] to bring forth, beget, produce.' …[N]o entity can be divorced from the notion of creativity. An entity is…capable of infusing its own particularity into creativity."[48]

Whitehead radically reimagined the concept of creativity as a relational activity. It became one of his more controversial ideas from a theological perspective because theologies of creation have often tied themselves to a specific view of God's power. For instance, the doctrine of creation-out-of-nothing (*creatio ex nihilo*) well exemplifies coercive power, for if God needs nothing to create whatever God wills, then it is the sheer force of God's will upon which the very

---

47. Weber, *Handbook of Whiteheadian Process Thought Volume 1*, 401.
48. Whitehead, *Process and Reality*, 213.

existence of all things depends. In contrast, a God whose essence is love creates relationally. That is, God opens the space for that which is other than God to freely participate in its own self-creation. Creativity, therefore, in this view need not be an exclusively divine attribute but rather the result of co-operation between God and the world.[49] Creation, in process thought, is always relational co-creation.

Whitehead further clarifies relational creativity as a threefold creative act, "composed of (i) the one infinite conceptual realization, (ii) the multiple solidarity of free physical realizations in the temporal world, (iii) the ultimate unity of the multiplicity of actual fact with the primordial conceptual fact."[50] The creative process begins with God's vision of beauty and goodness—the one infinite conceptual realization. In accordance with this vision, God presents relevant possibilities to every occasion. The world responds in freedom to realize or oppose these possibilities. Finally, God patiently receives into Godself the actualized facts of the world, saving what can be saved, and reconciling all the turmoil in accordance with the divine vision of beauty.

We can see therefore that God's act of creativity isn't one of force but one of persuasive and poetic cooperation. In relational creativity, God makes a fundamental renunciation of divine violence and coercive power. We can see the relevance to mimetic theory immediately, for it also renounces the idea of violence as being divinely

---

49. This is a key difference with Thomistic theology, which restricts creativity to God alone. Andrew M. Davis describes this creative process as follows: "The world requires God for its very possibility and God requires the world for the actualization of divine value." Andrew Davis, *Mind, Value, and Cosmos. On the relational nature of Ultimacy.* (Lanham, MD: Rowman & Littlefield 2021), 23. As such, creation is never out of nothing—another difference with classical Thomistic theology.

50. Whitehead, *Process and Reality*, 346.

sanctioned. Consequently, in both process and mimetic thought, humans, not God, are responsible for the violence in our world. The process philosopher and theologian, Andrew M. Davis, summarizes this big-picture view of co-creation:

> Far from being inferior, this vast relational vision crowns the world with ultimate significance and ultimate purpose; for God needs the world for the actualization of divine value. The world's actualization of this value thus reveals God to be "the mirror which discloses to every creature its own greatness." The world's "true destiny" is to be a "co-creator in the universe" and, thereby, find itself robed with "dignity" and "grandeur."[51]

Creativity, in relation to God, speaks to the persuasive influence and reconciling activities of God. The primacy of love in the nature of God, means that God's creative power is persuasive rather than coercive, poetic rather than forceful.[52] Relational creativity also means that God is affected by creation, receiving into Godself every moment, every experience, and every feeling. In this act of reception, everything is given context and meaning.

This context comes out of the universal past preserved in the memory of God and the future aim of beauty. Based on this teleological aim of the creation of beauty, the best possibilities for the next moment are presented to every "event" or entity. Within this vision of creativity, violence has no divine justification. In fact,

---

51. Davis, *Mind, Value, and Cosmos,* 207.

52. By implication, it means that God does not always get what God wants. The world, at any particular moment, is not all that God hoped it could be. Rather, God patiently and consistently draws it toward the ideal—the beauty that is possible for it.

violence can be seen as the failure of harmonization; violence misses the divine beauty to which every occasion is called.

Creativity, in relation to the world, refers to the uniqueness of every process of actualization. Every entity can be understood as a harmonizing activity, consolidating all influences and choosing which possibilities to actualize. As mentioned before, this view of creativity gives the world ultimate significance and dignity, for it is in the world's creative unfolding that divine value becomes actualized. God's vision of beauty is realized in actual material reality—the Word becomes flesh. Yet at the same time this process conception also shows that the world is ultimately responsible for its actual state. This view of relational co-creativity highlights both dignity and responsibility.

Beauty

Let's look more closely at Whitehead's concepts of beauty and harmonization. We can consider the process of harmonization for the purpose of explanation, or we can consider it with a sense of appreciation. In the order of appreciation, the terms God and beauty become more appropriate terminology for communicating the meaning of process. For Whitehead, the creative process of harmonization has inherent value. This value derives from the fact that God's valuation of possibilities orients toward truth, beauty, and goodness.[53] God is the Alpha and Omega, the beginning and the end of every creative act.[54] The beginning, by providing every creature with an initial aim—an ideal of itself—in the process of its becoming. The end, in that every actual event becomes part of God

---

53. Whitehead, *Process and Reality*, 346.
54. Ibid., 344.

and becomes reconciled to his vision of beauty.[55] In every moment therefore, God gives him/herself as the "initial object of desire."[56] As these possibilities are actualized, value is realized, and the beauty of God's conceptual valuations are diffused in actual occasions. Beauty is the unveiling and actualization of this underlying value. Consequently, beauty "is a quality which finds its exemplification in actual occasions."[57]

To experience beauty requires an openness; a sense of wonder; it needs a faith that sees beyond the surface of things and perceives our interior connection with the whole of reality. Describing this orientation of faith, Whitehead states: "[it] is to know that in being ourselves we are more than ourselves: to know that our experience, dim and fragmentary as it is, ... sounds the utmost depths of reality."[58] In this statement, we can sense the enigmatic nature of beauty—it contains both vagueness and clarity, points to both what is and what could be—as an experience that extends beyond the boundary of self into a sense of wholeness that includes more than self.

Yet, however dim and fragmentary our experience of beauty, for Whitehead it contains the deepest reality of our world. The vagueness of wonder opens a new clarity of experience; the opaqueness of the surface allows us to see the harmonies below with greater vividness. The paradox lies in the fact that what we experienced initially hides a deeper reality—and only in allowing the surface to become opaque or vague can we see through to the underlying treasure. For instance, the quality that arrests our attention in Van Gogh's painting of an ordinary wheat field, is the fact that he unveils the living

---

55. Ibid., 346.
56. Ibid.
57. Whitehead, *Adventures of ideas*, 252.
58. Whitehead, *Science and the Modern World*, 18.

movements below the surface of the familiar. His art suggests that there is more than what meets the eye.

The underlying vividness of harmonies is what arrests our attention and attunes us to beauty. As such, beauty has degrees: "There are gradations in Beauty and in types of Beauty," says Whitehead. [59] He also stresses that the degree of beauty is influenced by the "massiveness" and "intensity" of its harmonies.[60] *Massiveness* refers to the sheer scope or number of elements, and *intensity* refers to the depth of the harmony achieved. And so, for Whitehead, the aim of beauty in every occasion is twofold: first, the absence of inhibition. The various elements must retain their spontaneity of expression and not inhibit one another. With this goal achieved, "there is the minor form of beauty, the absence of painful clash."[61] Second, and with what Whitehead calls the major form of beauty, new contrasts and new harmonizations are created. This evokes a new intensity of feeling: "Thus the parts contribute to the massive feeling of the whole, and the whole contributes to the intensity of feeling of the parts."[62] The freedom of contrasting elements gives vibrancy to beauty.

Whitehead presents us with a vision of a wild and free cosmos. How does a God who neither controls nor coerces, get all these free entities to cooperate in creating beauty? Various words have been used to describe this persuasive influence: luring; calling; drawing; seducing. And maybe *seducing* would not be too strong a term to describe how beauty awakens desire in those called to an intimate flow of co-creation.

---

59. Whitehead, *Adventures of Ideas*, 252

60. Ibid., 253.

61. Ibid.

62. Ibid., 252.

For Whitehead, what he calls *appetition* defines the general unrest in every moment, the urge within every entity to transcend itself. Appetition is a form of desire evoked by the difference between what is and what might be. Whitehead connects this urge to the presence of God: "God's immanence in the world in respect to his primordial nature is an urge towards the future based upon an appetite in the present."[63] The very presence of God awakens desire and seduces creation with the possibility of greater beauty. Desire permeates all of existence and constitutes the reason the cosmos evolves rather than remains static. Desire can be understood as that feeling within every creature that greater satisfaction awaits. It can be as simple as the feeling of thirst or as complex as the human desire to participate in the beauty and purposes of God. [64]

Beauty awakens desire in entities because it offers itself as an intensification of experience. As we have seen, by their very nature, self-unifying entities participate in the beauty of harmonization. In choosing possibilities of beauty, every drop of experience intensifies its own satisfaction and simultaneously enhances the experience of God. Again, it's good to remind ourselves this "beauty" represents not some static goal or a final destination, but manifests instead as a vibrant beauty, finding life in diversity and intensification. As Whitehead noted, "The primordial appetitions which jointly constitute God's purpose are seeking intensity, and not preservation."[65] Consequently, entities are never permanently satisfied. Rather, every satisfaction makes way for the awakening of new desires, which lead to ever greater depths of satisfaction.

---

63. Whitehead, *Process and Reality,* 32.

64. "Thirst is an appetite towards a difference—towards something relevant, something largely identical, but something with a definite novelty." Ibid.

65. Ibid., 105.

In process thought, every part of creation participates in this diversification and intensification of experience and collectively becomes part of the fulfillment of God's own being. Whitehead continues: "His aim for it is depth of satisfaction as an intermediate step towards the fulfillment of his own being. His tenderness is directed towards each actual occasion, as it arises. Thus, God's purpose in the creative advance is the evocation of intensities."[66] The philosopher Elizabeth Kraus so eloquently rephrases Whitehead:

> By providing the data for divine physical feeling, the world brings about the concreteness of God, ransoming him from his abstract conceptual solitude, giving him matter to be woven into divine Flesh, objects to be illumined in divine consciousness, values to be purified by divine redemption. God is what the world makes him to be; the world is what God lures and redeems it to be. "Either of them... is the instrument of novelty for the other" (PR 349); "each is all in all" (PR 348), the all-ness of physical enjoyment everlastingly unified with the all-ness of conceptual appetition, thus perpetually satisfying the endless yearning of the creativity: "that all may be one." "For the kingdom of heaven is with us today" (PR 351).[67]

Beauty always seeks to harmonize diverse and complex factors into vibrant contrast within a unified self rather than creating conflicting oppositions. A harmonizing union amongst these diverse and contrasting factors means beauty has triumphed! But occasionally,

---

66. Ibid.

67. Elizabeth Kraus, *The Metaphysics of Experience* (American Philosophy) (New York: Fordham University Press, 2018), 240.

beauty remains unrealized and conflicts emerge. Occasions where beauty fails to happen are exactly where we need *salvation*. Salvation, from a process perspective, means that God receives these conflictual or unrealized experiences into Godself and attempts to place them within a larger context that still results in a beautiful whole. God saves all that can be saved. As Whitehead states: "The consequent nature of God is his judgment on the world. He saves the world as it passes into the immediacy of his own life. It is the judgment of a tenderness which loses nothing that can be saved."[68] For Whitehead, God's own desire for beauty and goodness forms the basis for this salvific trajectory within the cosmic story.

Despite the openness of reality, we can find a direction to its evolution. Not every event aims in the same direction because freedom remains real in an open cosmos, but we can see a cumulative trajectory that aims at beauty. Beauty expands and intensifies within our cosmic history. There are degrees of creativity and degrees of novelty. It may be difficult to recognize the novelty in every moment. Yet, every moment is a unique creative occurrence, even if no novelty can be discerned. Every event is an act of interpreting the past, anticipating the future, and choosing the most satisfying possibilities for actualization. In this sense, therefore, for Whitehead every event is a creative advance that adds to reality no matter how small the degree of novelty.

However, if we expand our perspective over a larger timespan, the reality of novelty and its trajectory becomes more obvious. For instance, the early stages of our universe consisted of simple gasses. If one could have observed this formless chaos, we would have had to stretch the imagination to envision galaxies of stars and planets,

---

68. Whitehead, *Process and Reality,* 346.

not to mention butterflies and bees. The emergence of life marks an obvious novel advance in this cosmic narrative. So, the indiscernible novelty that occurs in every moment of becoming accumulates over time in surprising ways.

The unfolding of the cosmic story reveals an inner dimension of meaning.[69] This story has a trajectory, however wild and free it may be. As events unfold, meaning accumulates.[70] The overall narrative moves toward beauty, diversity, and greater consciousness. In all its varied twists and turns, the flux of processes increases in complexity while always enriching its narrative meaning. We can hear a voice in the story of our cosmos. It whispers in every encounter; beckons in every event.

Whitehead recognizes this cosmic call and identifies it as beauty. He sees the development of civilizations to be a steady movement from force to persuasion.[71] The consistency of God's goodness, the beauty of God's vision, and the persistence of God's love have a directional affect upon the cosmic story and God's own story. Meaning evolves in the direction of beauty, and this trajectory serves as a testament to the nature of God. Each event participates in a larger story. Human experience takes place within a biographical context, and the narratives we construct are influenced by our experiences. The transformation of meaning, therefore, forms an essential factor in the journey toward beauty.

---

69. "I argue that we cannot expect to understand well what is going on in cosmic history apart from a careful examination of what goes on in the interior striving of life that reaches the summit of its intensity in humanity's spiritual adventures." Ibid., 1-2.

70. The process philosopher and theologian Charles Hartshorne spoke of creation as a cumulative process, a growing totality. See Charles Hartshorne, *Creative Experiencing: A Philosophy of Freedom*, ed. Donald Wayne Viney and Jincheal O. (Albany, NY: SUNY Press, 2012), 85.

71. Whitehead, Alfred. N. Chapter V. "From Force to Persuasion." In *Adventures of ideas*. (New York: Free Press, 1967).

3

Becoming Human: An Origin Story

There would be no human mind, no education, no transmission of culture without mimesis....The intense capacity of humans to imitate is what forces them to become what they are, but this capacity carries a high price.

—René Girard[1]

Imitative Origins

This second story, which I am basing on Rene Girard's insights about how we became human, takes us back a few hundred thousand years. We find the earth bursting with a myriad of life forms, each competing fiercely for survival. Major environmental changes, such as the expansion of savannas and the availability of food, cause some species to go extinct, while others prove more adaptable. Among these is a species of hominid that exhibits remarkable adaptability, allowing them to spread and survive across a wide area.

---

1. Girard, *Evolution and Conversion*, 56.

Girard gives us some basic outlines for how we may have become human from these early ancestors (a process he calls *hominization*). From there, we can imagine the stages that must have happened. In our scenario, significantly, some members of this group develop a novel capacity that sets them apart from other hominids. While most can pick up projectiles and throw them, this group does something surprisingly new. They repeat the action, practicing and imitating each other, ultimately becoming highly skilled in the behaviors they mimic. This increased capacity for imitation, or mimesis, proves to be advantageous in their harsh environment. In particular, becoming proficient in throwing projectiles allows them to kill their prey without entering the animal's dangerous perimeter, thus avoiding injury and death on many occasions. Moreover, the range of their bodily movements evolve differently because of this novel capacity to imitate.[2] These new mimetic abilities open up a whole new world of possibilities for this family of hominid, making them more adaptable to their environments and allowing them to adapt the environment to their needs for survival.

In our emergent human origins story, suppose this new complexity of imitative capacity in our hominid population need not remain limited to bodily behavior. Their appetites, passions, mental activity, and social interactions also undergo a complexification. Observing another to imitate actions suggests a new awareness of the distinction between *self* and *other*. Initially these new behaviors are driven by unconscious processes, but it also suggests the beginning of the emergence of a primitive self-awareness. And a new level

---

2. "Mimesis meant that hominids could repeat a movement or action, which sounds simple enough. However, this is exactly what is not found in other mammals, especially if you are looking for intentional action, such as practicing throwing." Vern Neufeld Redekop and Thomas Ryba, eds., *René Girard and Creative Mimesis*. (Lanham, MD: Lexington Books, 2016), 54.

of self-awareness opens up the possibility of a deeper relational connection with the other who is like self. Consequently, relational connection becomes even more complex and intense.[3]

These hominid's passions are no longer energized by instinctual appetites alone; instead, their intensified mimetic capacity allows desires to become mobile. Slowly but surely, they break free from instinctual boundaries with surprising consequences. Freedom and creativity abound. Communities become more complex. We are speaking here, though, of a community still dominated by an alpha. When a dominant animal rules a primitive community, violence is sporadic and relatively well-controlled. (The dominant animal grabs whatever it desires, and the rest makes do with whatever is left.) Occasionally the alpha's dominance might be tested. However, with the proliferation of desire, conflict increases. All these newfound capacities have a darker side as well. The intensity of conflict mirrors the development of mimetic abilities.

Although in this imaginative scenario we see only the first traces of self-awareness emerging, it already influences a sense of identity. Not only is group identity essential for survival in this environment, but we see the early flickers of individual identity beginning to emerge too. When passion increases and feelings intensify, an inevitable awareness of the interiority of those feelings becomes more acute. I want to draw attention to the creativity, novelty, and complexity of mental capacities produced by the process of mimesis itself.

---

3. Jesuit Theologian Raymund Schwager, one of Girard's interlocutors about theology, presents a number of scenarios in which he demonstrates how the intensity and complexity of relationship could have evolved. See Raymund Schwager, S. J., *Banished From Eden: Original Sin and Evolutionary Theory in the Drama of Salvation.* (Leominster, Herefordshire, UK: Gracewing, 2006,) 95.

Many Girardian scholars have emphasized the scapegoating process, which we will examine in the next part of our story, as the most significant generative human event. However, notice that the intensification of mimetic capacities is prior to, and more foundational than, the violence to come. Girard himself states: "violence does not play a primordial role in my perspective; only mimesis does. This point is often misunderstood."[4] The authors of the Genesis origin account share the same intuition, when they define humanity in terms of their reflective capacity—beings created in the image and likeness of God (Genesis 1:26). And the Yahwist origin accounts of Genesis 2 and 3 also imagine a period of creative development, of the awakening of desire, and the complexification of relationship to precede the first act of violence.

But to return to our narrative: greater intensity of feeling has consequences. When intense passions are frustrated, they erupt, and these eruptions become so chaotic and violent that the dominant animal can no longer control the violence. We can see how the communal structure could break down, status boundaries disappear, and passions run wild in a violent frenzy of all against all. Girard speculates that many proto-human communities destroyed themselves in this way, and those communities that survived were severely damaged by the losses.

The evolution of these new mimetic capacities gave significant advantages and simultaneously introduced great danger to these hominids. In our story, for thousands of years, these events replay themselves. Uncontrolled violence becomes a seemingly insurmountable obstacle to advancement. The unconscious yearning for a solution intensifies. How can these proto-humans retain the

---

4. Burkert, Walter, et al. *Violent Origins.* (Stanford University Press, 1999), 123.

advantages yet reduce the danger inherent in the evolution of their mimetic capacities? They need a catalyst, a revolution that can push them over the brink of this obstacle.

A Creative Leap

Then it happens. As Girard imagines it, a community at some point finds itself in the familiar scenario of escalating tension again. Frustrations grow. All the members feel it, but they don't know why the escalation of conflict is happening or how to stop it. For them, the movements of desire are unconscious, and the consequent chaos is mysterious. Then suddenly one of its members snaps and kills another. This unleashes retributive violence. Tension grows. Will this be another frenzy of violence, everyone turning on everyone else? The group is swept along as if by an unseen yet irresistible current. However, something unforeseen happens; at the very moment when the group is about to descent into uncontrolled and violent cathartic release, one of the community members points to another. The source of the frustration is suggested by this gesture. Violence finds a focus. A crowd converges upon a single victim. One dies instead of many. Girard identifies this spontaneous process as scapegoating, although the etymological origins of the word would develop later.[5]

Girard speculates how when the blind passion subsides and the violence ceases, the chaotic noise makes way for a moment of silent attention. In this flicker of contemplation, everyone glimpses a symbol that overflows with meaning: the corpse of their victim: One that was in the community is now out; yet this death means life for the remaining community. Chaos has been transformed into order by this dead body. This scapegoating process will be repeated

---

5. For a history of the idea see David Dawson, *Flesh Becomes Word: A Lexicography of the Scapegoat or, the History of an Idea*. (East Lansing: Michigan State University Press, 2013).

incalculable times, and each time the symbol will grow in significa-
tion until reaching a threshold that radically moves symbolic
thought onto a new foundation.

The gesture of pointing of the finger, of accusation, would set in
motion such a significant process that it would be experienced as a
palpable presence. The Hebrew Bible names this process, *the satanos.*
The word *satanos* is not a name but a noun. As such it is often used
with the definite article as in "the" accuser, "the" adversary, "the"
stumbling block. However, over time, Girard believes this process
played such a substantial role in human development that it took on
a personality of almost ontological reality. Girard explains: Satan is
imagined and symbolized as a person, as "someone," because satanic
power becomes attached to the victim as the victim mechanism does
its work. The victim is viewed as a devil or demon.[6] It is significant
to note that the very symbol of evil emerges out of the scapegoating
process. As we'll see later, when the process gets exposed, the symbol
will be transformed as well.

Complex Symbolic Thought

In Girard's thought, the mimetic cycles and the scapegoating mechanism are not processes which humans invented but rather, the very
processes that made us human. These evolutionary events transformed animals into humans by providing the possibility for complex symbolic thought and language. Scientists know that animals
do have a primitive culture in the form of co-operation and tool-
making. However, they lack complex symbols. Some of the great
apes have been taught the meaning of basic words. They know, for
instance, that a.p.p.l.e. refers to a certain kind of fruit. But none

6. Girard, René. *I See Satan Fall Like Lightning.* (Orbis Books, 2012,) 88.

could be taught the symbolic meaning of "you are the apple of my eye." An excess of meaning in our symbolic thought and language seems to be unique to humankind.[7] For Girard, the corpse of the scapegoat serves precisely as the *kind* of symbol that contains such an excess of meaning that it can serve as the catalyst for the emergence of the uniquely human, complex symbolic thought.[8]

The very possibility of meaning relies on the recognition of differences. Girard shows how the chaos that precedes the act of scapegoating violence represents a crisis of undifferentiation. At this stage of the crisis, rationality does not guide the frenzied mob; an irrational act of violence brings a cathartic end to the chaos. We have here a moment of possibility: a moment in which their irrational passions are satisfied thereby creating room to consider the meaning of the moment. Mindless rage gives way to focused wonder. In no other event might opposites become as intense and obvious as in the corpse of the scapegoat. It symbolizes the death that brought life; the chaos that brought order; the violence that brought peace; the outcast and the community; the curse and the blessing; the demonic and the divine. I would suggest that maybe this was the first moment in which we vaguely heard the appeal of "the lamb slain from the foundation of the world" (Revelation 13:8), to our conscience. Or more precisely, the innocence of our victim created an opportunity for *conscience*, a sense of right and wrong, to emerge.

---

7. "Chimpanzees and a few other animals are capable of symbolic thought, but they are not very good at it. It is not an exercise that comes to them easily or spontaneously. Extensive sustained training is required before these animals can learn to use but a few symbols in a highly artificial 'prepared' environment that has been created precisely for that purpose. Humans, on the other hand, do it spontaneously; 'naturally' one would say." Alison, *The Palgrave Handbook of Mimetic Theory and Religion*, 15.

8. The philosopher Paul Dumouchel observes: "Girard's elegant and original solution is to start from an undefined, exceedingly significant single symbol, which signifies precisely through the excess of significations that it contains." Alison, *The Palgrave Handbook of Mimetic Theory and Religion*, 17.

The recent discovery of mirror neurons in primates underscores the intensification of mimetic capacities in their evolution.[9] As observed before, a new level of mimetic capacity also enables a new level of conflict. Basic forms of scapegoating have been observed amongst primates. Scapegoating therefore seems to be a natural and important step toward limiting uncontrolled violence, toward increasing co-operation, and toward the beginnings of culture. Girard presents his argument as follows:

> We have to show that the intensification of mimetic rivalry, which is already very much in evidence at the level of primates, destroyed dominance patterns and gave rise to progressively more elaborate and humanized forms of culture through the intermediary of the surrogate victim. At the point when mimetic conflict becomes sufficiently intense to prohibit the direct solutions that give rise to the forms of animal sociality, the first 'crisis' or series of crises would then occur as the mechanism that produces the differentiated, symbolic, and human forms of culture.[10]

Girard posits the corpse of the scapegoat as the original symbol, and so for him this entails that violence has shaped the very capacities humans have in the process of meaning-making. Concepts of the *sacred*, of *sacrifice*, of violence, and of the divine originate here for Girard. Wrathful gods who delight in sacrifice and justify our violence find their origin in this event, or rather, in the misinterpretation of this event. This leads to a startling conclusion: If we were

---

9. See Scott R. Garrels, *Mimesis and Science: Empirical Research on Imitation and the Mimetic Theory of Culture and Religion.* (East Lansing: Michigan State University Press, 2011).
10. Girard, *Things Hidden since the Foundation of the World,* 94.

to have any hope of transforming these concepts, we would have to revisit the event that birthed them and reinterpret the symbol in which they originate.

The Birth of a New Community

Our story now progresses from a scenario involving pre-human hominids and the process of hominization to early human communities. Girard speculates that uncontrolled violence destroyed many primitive communities. However, the scapegoating process introduced a new kind of violence—what he calls a sacred violence—for it saves the community from the uncontrolled violence. In primitive communities where there are no laws to limit violence, conflict easily escalates. When at the height of mimetic crisis, the crowd becomes united in their accusations against a scapegoat, it brings about a new unity within the community. Rivals become friends when they share a common enemy. In expelling or murdering the scapegoat they experience a cathartic release and a seemingly "magical" peace descends upon the community. Magical, because they don't recognize the true nature of the process that made this peace possible.[11] In the same way they identified the scapegoat as the reason for all the chaos, they now identify it as the reason for the peace. Consequently, the community deifies the scapegoat. All the elements necessary for the birth of a new community, a new beginning, and a new sense of the *sacred* become present in this "saving" event. Girard states:

---

11. A misunderstanding of mimesis often gives birth to a belief in magic. For instance: "Early anthropologists perceived something of the religious character of mimesis and spoke of imitative magic; for instance, many primitives guard against having clippings of their hair or nails fall into the hands of potential adversaries." Girard, *Things Hidden Since the Foundation of the World*, 14.

Thus, there is at least one moment in which peace is restored within the community, and the community never praises itself for this reconciliation; it regards this new acquisition of order as a gift from the victim it just killed. This is both malefic because it caused the crisis, but also beneficial because its death restored peace, and therefore the scapegoat becomes divinized in the archaic sense, that is, the all-powerful, Almighty both for good and for bad simultaneously.[12]

A community that had found itself in the clutches of a chaotic monster, about to be devoured by uncontrolled violence, now finds itself born anew into a new unity and a new peace. It's not hard to see why Girard proposes this event as foundational in the formation of civilizations. It's important to note as well that Girard refers not to just one specific event that happens one time, but a series of events that forms a pattern and accumulates meaning over time.

We recognize the practice of scapegoating because it still happens on so many levels within our families, communities, and nations. Yet few before Girard recognized the significant anthropological role it played in the formation of civilizations. If indeed these events of scapegoating violence were foundational for human development, in structuring our brains and social interactions, then we cannot simply hastily glance over them and move on to consider the more positive aspects of human rationality. Our history has shown again and again that if you place good and rational people in the right situation, they become capable of committing unimaginable acts of violence. Our rationality has not completely mastered the unconscious passions that formed us. In fact, we often still employ our

---

12. Girard, *Evolution and Conversion*, 48.

rationality in the service of justifying our passions. This brings me to an inevitable conclusion: our beliefs or rationality alone cannot save us from our violent origins (an ideal with which Girard would concur); rather, we need a deep transformation of our desires, or more accurately, the source of our desires.

Ritual and Myth

Let's return to our archaic scenario. What happened next, after the scapegoating event and its mystification? For the effect and meaning of the scapegoating mechanism to continue, the community needs to remember the event. And the best way of remembering in a pre-literate age will be through re-enactment. Consequently, rituals develop.[13] The ritualistic repetition of the scapegoating violence forms the basis for religious sacrifice.

Imagine being part of such a primitive community and the events that lead to scapegoating. We don't want the violence so destructive of our community to erupt again, and we also don't want to suffer the same fate as our victim. How do we protect ourselves? We might ask, what caused the victim to suffer this fate? For whatever caused the violence should be avoided! Because we are unwilling to see ourselves as the cause of the victim's suffering, we look for other causes. In our blindness we soon identify the causes of the victim's punishment: it must be certain actions, words, and objects that defiled the victim and caused purity to demand revenge. As we have seen, the scapegoat's corpse probably serves as the first and most universally

---

13. "There are two possible views of ritual. On the one hand, the Enlightenment view for which religion is superstition and if ritual is everywhere, it's because cunning and avid priests impose their abracadabras on the good people. On the other hand, if we simply consider that the clergy cannot really precede the invention of culture, then religion must come first and far from being a derisory farce, it appears as the origin of the whole culture. And humanity is the child of religion." Alison, *The Palgrave Handbook of Mimetic Theory and Religion*, 80.

revered source of defilement. Moreover, the associated objects and actions that lead up to the final murder soon become "taboos" as well.[14] Over time, different communities develop a great diversity of taboos in different religions. What might be sacred in one might be meaningless in another. An object's sacred status will be determined by its presence in the events that led up to the final violence. Thus, we find a great diversity in religious practices, yet the actual practice of sacrifice is universal in archaic religions.

We can conclude that religions might have great diversity in their reasoning and speculation about what caused these violent events, but despite the diversity of rituals and origin myths, all point to a common, culminating event of sacred violence. Oral and later written myths or sacred stories will play a complimentary role to rituals. Many origin myths follow the pattern of a story of mimetic crisis that gives birth to chaotic monsters and a creative act of violence that saves the community from annihilation. As each community develops their own myths, rituals, and religious traditions, a multitude of gods are created in the image and likeness of that community.[15]

There's one big problem: because what Girard calls the scapegoating mechanism results from a misinterpretation of the problem

---

14. "According to mimetic theory, myths are narratives of those violent crises, rites are repetitions of the behaviors that brought the crisis to an end, and taboos are attempts to prevent crises by prohibiting behaviors that might have incited them." (Ibid., 320.)

15. "We can hypothetically assume that several prehistoric groups did not survive precisely because they didn't find a way to cope with the mimetic crisis; their mimetic rivalries didn't find a victim who polarized their rage, saving them from self-destruction. We could even conceive of groups that solved one or two crises through the founding murder but failed to re-enact it ritually, developing a durable religious system, and therefore succumbing to the next crisis. What I have said is that the threshold of culture is related to the scapegoat mechanism, and that the first known institutions are closely related to its deliberate and planned re-enactment....The old question of the anteriority of myth over ritual, or ritual over myth, is solved: ritual is the deliberate reproduction of the mechanism; myth is the narrative (inevitably distorted) of its origins." Girard, *Evolution and Conversion*, 113.

of violence, the effects wear off. The actual problem is twisted mimetic desire, bound to flare up again. But when a similar crisis befalls the community, they remember what saved them the previous time and their ritual re-enactment of the selection and sacrifice of a scapegoat becomes part of a cycle that preserves the community.

Religion and Civilization

As we have seen, Girard regards religion and culture not as the inventions of rational human beings but as essential processes in the evolution of humanity. For him, the scapegoating process functions as a catalyst in the development of symbolic thought. This increased mental capacity leads to ritual and myth, which in their turn develop into religion. A society that can control violence can then develop into a civilization. For Girard, ritual, myth, religion, and culture all intertwine. The scapegoating mechanism makes it all possible. (But remember, the scapegoating process is dependent on increased mimetic capacities). Consequently, at the foundation of every civilization lies a kind of tomb, a monument to what Girard calls the "founding murder." Even the pyramid, the above-ground tomb, he points out, did not need to be invented, for it is the shape of "the pile of stones in which the victim of unanimous stoning is buried. It is the first pyramid."[16]

When Girard first developed these ideas, it was popular to blame religion for violence. In contrast, Girard believed that religion does not cause violence, rather, violence causes religion. The problem of violence goes much deeper than any one belief system or

---

16. Girard, René. *Things Hidden since the Foundation of the World*, 83.

institution.[17] In fact, the human race births religion out of the need to contain violence. In this regard Girard says:

> One of the central points of the mimetic theory which could contribute a good deal to the debate, if we take it seriously, is that religion is the mother of culture. In the process of the emergence of cultural elements, one also needs to stress that there is no absolute beginning. The process is extremely complex and progressive.[18]

Long after the establishment of these early archaic societies, our more modern civilizations remain bound by the myths and violent mechanisms on which they were founded. Empires, for instance, sincerely believing in their divine right to domination, have taught their slaves using the Bible that slavery must be God's will and purpose. Nations, believing in their divine right to luxury, have persuaded their young men to sacrifice themselves in wars to guarantee their excessive way of life. In order to wash our hands of their blood, we convince ourselves that our victims either deserved their fate, or that they heroically volunteered to sacrifice themselves.

But when the one sacrificed becomes exposed as a victim, rather than a hero, the very foundations of the system founded on murder start to crumble. When the innocence of our victims and the guilt of the community is revealed, we no longer have a legitimate reason for their slaughter. This will be an important point for Girard theologically in his interpretation of the passion narratives of the

---

17. "For Girard, religion came into existence as an inter-individual, social solution to the problem of ubiquitous rivalry and violence in human groups." Alison, *The Palgrave Handbook of Mimetic Theory and Religion*, 58.

18. Girard, *Evolution and Conversion*, 70.

Gospels. He urges us to find a new foundation for our civilizations, lest they remain vulnerable to the violence that birthed them. Girard notes: "Christians heartily distrusted the sovereign states in which Christianity emerged and spread, on account of the violent origin of these states."[19] For Girard, Christianity and the revelation contained in the Hebrew Bible and New Testament play decisive roles in both the revealing of the victim and in the possibility of a new kind of community, not based on scapegoating.

Reinterpretation and Conversion

The narratives collected in the biblical scriptures began in the ancient Near East. These biblical stories have similar themes, characters, events, and structures to those of their neighbors. Canaan, Syria, Mesopotamia and to some degree, Egypt, shared a similar culture. Smaller tribes within the larger culture developed unique versions of common stories. Yet, despite their similarities, Girard believes the Hebrew scriptures begin to offer something radically new. Girard sees the biblical scriptures as a progressive deconstruction of the myths of culture (stories which Girard says are always told from the point of view of the persecutor), revealing our own troubled relationship with violence and sacrifice. He summarizes the Biblical anthropological revelation as follows:

> The mimetic anthropology is devoted both to the acknowledgement of the mimetic nature of desire and to the unfolding of the social consequences of this knowledge, to the revelation of the innocence of the victim and to the

---

19. Girard, *I See Satan Fall Like Lightning*, 95.

understanding that the Bible and the Gospels do it for us in advance.[20]

In the anthropological story we've developed so far, all the gods are creations of human beings, birthed in the misinterpretation of extreme experiences such as the tensions between violence and peace. The Bible does contain many aspects of this anthropological narrative: namely, it foregrounds the processes of mimetic desire, conflict, and scapegoating. However, new possibilities of meaning emerge in both the old and the new Testaments. The idea of *conversion* comes about because of a radical subversion of meaning we see as the narrative unfolds. Through the counter-intuitive transformation of meaning, the presence of the true God becomes implied—a God present in flesh.[21] Rather than manipulating our narrative from the outside, Girard shows how this God transforms meaning from the inside. From the process point of view we have explored before, we could say we have here a surprising yet powerful witness to a God that is both immanent and transcendent, intertwined with the world, yet calling it to transcend itself. We will speak more of this intersection in the next section.

Unlike other interpreters of myth such as Joseph Campbell, Girard didn't consider the Biblical narratives as simply another iteration of the same basic mythic story. Rather, he shows how the Biblical text deconstructs the origin myths themselves, shows the

---

20. Girard, *Evolution and Conversion,* 141.

21. "For the moment it is possible to say in short order that it is exactly the semiotic shift that Girard presents which makes the whole thing work. It is precisely as a semiotic reversal of the sacred that the biblical reading is introduced. And thus, the very existence of the shift—its textual and semiotic dynamic—'creates' the meaning of a nonviolent divine." Anthony Bartlett, *Theology Beyond Metaphysics: Transformative Semiotics of René Girard.* (Eugene, OR: Cascade Books, 2020), 49.

foundation on which they are built. He concedes that to decon-struct myth, the biblical stories must have some aspects in common with myth to expose what is false. Girard draws this distinction: "In biblical monotheism we cannot suspect God of being the product of the scapegoat processes that quite visibly produce the gods in primitive polytheism."[22] The nonviolent God revealed in the Judeo-Christian scriptures has a different origin, he argues, untainted by scapegoating and human violence.

Girard shows how whereas myth hides the truth of the scape-goating mechanism and the innocence of the victim, the biblical scriptures begin to reveal it. This happens gradually, but it starts right at the beginning. For instance, the Bible also affirms, like the myths, that the first civilization began with a founding death—yet, instead of calling it a sacrifice, the Bible names it for what it is: a murder which founded a civilization. "Cain attacked his brother Abel and killed him" (Genesis 4:8). "Cain was then building a city, and he named it after his son Enoch" (v.17). Throughout his work, Girard demonstrates how a radical self-critique of the practice of sacrifice and repudiating the role of God in violence permeates the scriptures. Making this distinction between myth and Scripture clear, Girard writes:

> The myth and the biblical story are in basic opposition over the decisive question that collective violence poses: Is it war-ranted? Is it legitimate? In the myth the expulsions of the hero are justified each time. In the biblical account they never are. Collective violence is unjustifiable.[23]

---

22. Girard, *I See Satan Fall Like Lightning*, 107.
23. Ibid., 108-109.

Another striking example of the subversion of the meaning of myth can be found in Genesis 1. Most scholars recognize the similarity of the Genesis 1 creation story and the Near East myth of Enuma Elish. The stories have a similar beginning and structure, namely: God begins creating. There is chaos. But then the bible introduces a surprising twist. Chaos is not overcome by violence, as in Enuma Elish, but by the spirit of Elohim hovering over the deep. God creates order out of chaos with a word, rather than with violence. So for Girard, the bible offers new possibilities of meaning in a world where violence has seemed to be the only solution.

Girard argues that the human story finds a crescendo in the story of Jesus, as his message and life becomes the most comprehensive subversion of myth. The biblical narrative does not simply reproduce the symbols and meanings of myth but progressively subverts them. And I will argue that subversion requires an entering in, an intimate familiarity with the subject, so that it can be transformed from the inside out. We can see how something truly new and creative unfolds in the biblical narrative. This progression in the narrative, this openness to new possibilities of meaning, I see as a profound affirmation of a God who is open; a God who invites us to realize greater beauty and greater meaning; a God who uses persuasion rather than force. All this begins to sound consistent with the process God with whom we have already become acquainted. Girard articulates an "evolutionary" view of scripture, stating:

> Judaism, since its inception, is the absolute refusal of this god-fabricating machinery. In Judaism God has no relationship to victimization, and victims are no longer divinized. That is what we call revelation, which, historically, unfolds in two stages. First of all, there is a shift from myth to the

Bible, where, as I said, God is devictimized and the victims are dedivinized; then you have the full evangelic revelation. God experiences the role of victim, but this time deliberately, in order to free man from his violence.[24]

Girard has an evolutionary view not only of the emergence of human beings from animals, but of divine, loving involvement in our world. Even if he doesn't say so explicitly, the progression of the narrative makes it evident. God is part of the human drama, involved in the temporal cycles of human development. We will see other parallels with Whitehead's thought in the next section where I seek to harmonize them.

The Event of Jesus Christ

Girard sees the life and message of Jesus as an unveiling of the scapegoating mechanism, and as a new and true interpretation of the events that made us human. In Girard's own words:

> From an anthropological standpoint I would define Christian revelation as the true representation of what had never been completely represented or what had been falsely represented: the mimetic convergence of all against one, the single victim mechanism with its antecedent developments, particularly "interdividual" scandals.[25]

Girard's thought has profound theological implications. Recognizing the transformation of meaning throughout the scriptures

---

24. Girard, *Evolution and Conversion, 143.*
25. Girard, *I See Satan Fall Like Lightning,* 137.

proves essential in grasping the significance of Jesus Christ, who came in the fullness of time (Ephesians 1:10), to give us understanding (1 John 5:20), and unveil what was hidden since the foundation of the world (Matthew 13:35). For Girard, the hiddenness of the scapegoating mechanism forms the very foundation upon which the world order was established.[26]

The principles upon which our civilizations were (and in some ways still are) based would be exposed in the events of Jesus' life. Jesus' story summarizes the human story, then offers a conclusion that we were unable to reach ourselves before this moment. The circular events in which chaos gives way to order and order succumbs to chaos, the never-ending cycle of victors and victims has finally been interrupted by this truly new event. Jesus not only exposes the events and models that formed us, but provides us with a new model of what being human could mean. Girard explains:

> All archaic religions grounded their rituals precisely around the re-enactment of the founding murder. In other words, they considered the scapegoat to be guilty of the eruption of the mimetic crisis. By contrast, Christianity, in the figure of Jesus, denounced the scapegoat mechanism for what it actually is: the murder of an innocent victim, killed in order to pacify a riotous community. That's the moment in which the mimetic mechanism is fully revealed.
>
> ... Now, I think that the unconscious nature of sacrificial violence is revealed in the New Testament, particularly in Luke: 'Father, forgive them, for they do not know what they are doing' (Luke 23:34).

---

26. See the section "The Gospel Revelation of the Founding Murder," *Things Hidden since the Foundation of the World*, 158.

… Without the Cross, there is no revelation of the fundamental injustice of the scapegoat mechanism, which is the
founder of human culture, with all its repercussions in our
relationships with each other. [27]

Religion and culture developed by means of the scapegoating
mechanism, and to function they depend on the truth about the
mechanism being concealed. In contrast, Jesus came to reveal the
truth about the innocence of the victim. As such Jesus inaugurates
the end of religion.[28] We can see how the whole setting of Jesus'
story serves as a micro-cast of the human drama, of our conflicted
history. Once again, the archaic story we looked at gets reenacted:
Israel once again finds herself in subjection to a pagan empire—the
Roman Empire. Within the Jewish nation there are numerous fac-
tions and competing voices. In the midst of the frustration, the desire for deliverance intensifies. Many would-be messiahs have raised
their voices in the thick of these tensions and incited the crowds.
Most of these would-be saviors met a violent end. The gospels all
seem to race toward the last week of Jesus' life and death. Multiple
conflicts, plots, and schemes converge in this last week, one in which
all these frustrations fuse and become focused on one culprit.

Within this chaotic environment Jesus' teaching and actions
are starting to make people nervous. The religious authorities have
also noticed him and grow increasingly offended at his teaching and
popularity. He constantly steps beyond the accepted boundaries,
embracing outcasts and thus blurring the social differences. All these

---

27. Girard, *Evolution and Conversion*, 157.

28. "Religion performs an essential service for the community. But the religion is of course
based on a lie, namely the supposed guilt of the victim." Michael Kirwan, In *Girard and
Theology*. (London: T & T Clark, 2009), 67.

events race toward the Passover feast when Jews from all over the region would flock to Jerusalem. We have all the elements for conflict present: national tensions, religious zeal, and personal frustrations. Individuals, families, and nations seem to be obliviously swept along currents of conflict. Everything we have been unaware of, including the unconscious processes upon which we have built our identities and founded our communities—the realities we tried to hide with our myths—are what Jesus comes to make us conscious of.

We saw earlier how the process of accusations—our internal chaos and frustrated desires, misinterpreted as the guilt of the scapegoat—became personified in the symbol of *the satan*, or what the New Testament often refers to as the Devil. Scripture confirms that it is the event of the crucifixion that defeats the Devil (Hebrews 2:14). How? Notice how the closer the gospel narratives move to the actual passion event, the less visible the character of Satan becomes. Is it because the very form of the satanic is transformed in the process of its exposure? Indeed, it is the exposure of evil that defeats it. The principalities and powers would not have crucified the Lord if they knew what was happening (1 Cor. 2:8). The very principles on which our societies were founded, the powers by which they rule, would be unveiled in this event. When Jesus says, "I see Satan fall like lightning" (Luke 10:18), it can be interpreted as: I see the mythical personification of evil exposed as the very earthly process of accusation.

The original symbol that birthed our concepts of gods, of ourselves, and of sacrifice—the symbol that made symbolic thought itself possible—will be reinterpreted and radically subvert human meaning. In the Gospel stories, history repeats in the sequence of events in which conflict intensifies as the Jewish nation fights for its survival, and Rome relies on its trusted method of violence to rule.

These tensions eventually resolve as all rivals melt together into a united voice of condemnation.

In this dramatic scene, Jesus becomes the chosen scapegoat. He enters into the heart of our myth by becoming the victim and from there, he exposes the myth. Girard stresses repeatedly that the true God does not participate in our cycles of violence but calls us to transcend them. This God does not justify our violence but suffers it. This God does not demand violence, but in the midst of suffering, offers forgiveness. Jesus strips the principalities and powers bare—the principles by which we have governed and exercised power in human communities have been founded upon a lie. Light finally shines on the practice of sacrifice in this event of the perfect sacrifice, and the truth it reveals brings an end to the justification of violent sacrifice.[29] We continue to see these ideas developed further in the New Testament theology and reported events. The Apostle Paul's conversion, for instance, finds its basis on the revelation of his participation in the persecutory process.[30] Being part of the cycles of violence distorts our vision of both others and ourselves, whether we be victims or perpetrators of violence.

Theological Possibilities

One of the first questions presented in the present work was whether open and relational theological ideas were implicit in Girard's

---

29. Michael Kirwin notes that Girard's seismic impact on the theory of atonement derives from his devastating suspicion and critique of sacrifice. Girard later accepted that there is a place for sacrifice language in a radically subverted form. See Kirwan, Michael and Sheelah T. Hidden, eds., *Mimesis and Atonement: René Girard and the Doctrine of Salvation.* (London: Bloomsbury Academic 2018), 115. See also: Mark S. Heim, *Saved from Sacrifice: A Theology of the Cross.* (Grand Rapids, MI: Eerdmans, 2008).

30. "The question Paul hears is crucial: 'Saul, why do you persecute me?' (Acts 22.7). This is the fundamental question. Christian conversion is our discovery that we are persecutors without knowing it. All participation in the scapegoat phenomenon is the same sin of the persecution of Christ. And all human beings commit this sin." (Girard, *Evolution and Conversion,* 142).

mimetic theory. From a Girardian perspective, the gods born from violence are nothing more than projections of those who perpetrate violence; idols that reflect the misunderstandings of humanity in its infancy, grasping for meaning.

Here we begin to come to a significant intersection between process thought and Girardian mimetic thought. The popular concept of God, as an entity that has absolute power and controls world events, loses its persuasiveness in the light of these anthropological revelations. Such a god simply does not exist in Girardian anthropology. Instead, an alternative vision of God emerges. This God does not control but patiently works in the background, present in every moment, opening new possibilities of meaning. Even when humanity misunderstood events, sinking to the depths of violence, this God has drawn the story forward, not by external force, but by the persistent influence of the divine vision of beauty and goodness.

We've seen how as Girard's anthropological story develops, and violence and twisted mimetic desire are progressively exposed, a new vision of God also comes to light. Girard might not have emphasized this, but for me the story reaches a crescendo in the event of Jesus where God is unveiled as the one who suffers our violence rather than the one justifying it. This progression in the story leads to a type of conversion. The Bible does not explicitly state what we should believe concerning God. Rather its central aim is to expose the violent origin of our meaning-making capacities and at the same time offer us a new basis for creating meaning. It is this new possibility, this radical transformation of the very structure of meaning, that points to the nature of God. We can find in these stories a profound affirmation of a God who is open; a God who invites us to realize greater beauty and greater meaning; a God who uses persuasion rather than force.

4

Processing Mimetic Desire

Mimetic Nature

We've already established that mimetic capacities (or prehension within the process schema) have found a new level of intensity and complexity within humans. Mimesis, in a Girardian context, describes a specific relationship, a process of imitation. The words *imitate, mimic, mimesis* and *mimetic* all have similar etymological origins. Girard himself preferred the word *mimesis* above the term *imitation* because he thought there was less conscious awareness in mimesis than what was typically meant by imitation.[1] So for Girard, mimesis represents an unconscious form of imitation. However, because we are unveiling the process and bringing it into conscious awareness, the use of the word *imitation* can be appropriate at times as well. One can find the mimetic process woven into every aspect of our humanity, including our cultures, our religions, and our economies. Mimesis proves so fundamental to what makes us human that Girard writes: "The intense capacity of humans to imitate is what forces them to become what they are."[2]

---

1. Girard, *Evolution and Conversion*, 44.
2. Girard, *Evolution and Conversion*, 56.

Whitehead, too, recognized this ability to imitate or *reproduce* as a key factor in the evolution of humanity. For our ancient ancestors, the daily strain of survival produced intense feelings. Art originated as they "reproduce a vivid experience flashed out among the necessities of daily life."[3] For Whitehead, what separates art from the initial, actual experience is the freedom with which they could re-live the feeling without the immediacy of the danger and strain. Thus, art originates in "the simple craving to enjoy freely the vividness of life which first arises in moments of necessity."[4] Girard does not speculate about why the mimetic capacity intensified in our ancestors. Whitehead shows that all of nature is a creative advance to intensify experience. Thus, the very capacity for imitation is founded in the desire to reproduce experiences and enjoy the vividness of life without the immediacy of danger that was present at first.

Girard emphasizes that this mimetic capacity should be understood as foundational to our humanity. Our most sophisticated capacities, such as language, depend on our ability to imitate. We don't learn to imitate; rather we learn by imitating.[5] It is an ability so basic to our humanity that it functions on an instinctual level and consequently, it is often blind to itself.[6] Studies of childhood development confirm as much, demonstrating that newborn babies can imitate facial expressions.[7]

---

3. Whitehead, *Adventures of Ideas*. 272.

4. Ibid.

5. See Garrels, *Mimesis and Science*.

6. Alison, *The Palgrave Handbook of Mimetic Theory and Religion*, 22.

7. Andrew N. Meltzoff and Keith M. Moore. "Explaining Facial Imitation: A Theoretical Model." *Infant and Child Development* 6, no. 3-4, 1997: 179-192.

In the last couple of decades we have seen a revival in the study of mimesis within scientific circles.[8] The discovery of mirror neurons, in particular, suggests the potential biological basis of our mimetic capacity. A number of scholars have explored the connection between imitation, mirror neurons, and mimetic desire.[9] Some process philosophers have recognized the potential relevance of mirror neurons to Whitehead's idea that experience in the form of *"feeling"* goes all the way down, even to an atomic level. Viney and Shields, for instance, argue that mirror neurons have significance for the process idea that emotional data transfers between occasions.[10] In the case of mirror neurons, emotional data transfer happens on a cellular level.

All this suggests that within a Girardian context, the concept of imitation entails much greater depth than simply "monkey see, monkey do." For mimesis represents the unconscious process of perceiving and duplicating the actual *interiority* of another person. As such, it has many implications and potential benefits that we don't normally associate with the word *imitation*. For instance, one can immediately see the evolutionary benefit of mentally duplicating the experience of another without expending the same energy. We can also see that both Whitehead's concept of prehensions and Girard's language of mimesis stress interiority, and the organism's appropriation of interiority.

---

8. See for instance: Garrels, *Mimesis and Science.*

9. See Garrels, S. R. (2005). Imitation, Mirror Neurons, and Mimetic Desire: Convergence Between the Mimetic Theory of René Girard and Empirical Research on Imitation. *Contagion: Journal of Violence, Mimesis, and Culture, 12*(1), 47–86. https://doi.org/10.1353/ctn.0.0004

10. Donald W. Viney and George W. Shields, *The Mind of Charles Hartshorne: A Critical Examination,* (Anoka, MN: Process Century Press. 2020), 100-102.

Mimetic Desire

Mimetic desire identifies the process by which we unconsciously reproduce the desires of others. Girard connects the uniqueness of human imitation/mimesis to the uniqueness of human desire.[11] From the earliest relational experiences of a baby following the eye movements of a parent, what is desirable is continually suggested to us by those we are in relationship with. We have stressed that mimetic desire functions on an unconscious level.[12] As a more mature sense of self develops, the process by which we imitate the desires of others becomes more hidden. It may be that the conscious self could not develop if this process was too visible.

Mimetic desire increases our capacity for both good and evil and is essential for a greater level of freedom. According to Girard, mimetic desire frees us from instinctual appetites. It enables us to open ourselves to others, to be influenced by them, and to learn skills and acquire knowledge.[13] The very mobility of mimetic desire is what frees us from a slavish subservience to instinct. Girard puts it this way:

"Only mimetic desire can be free, can be genuine desire, human desire, because it must choose a model more than the object itself. Mimetic desire is what makes us human, what

---

11. "Desire is undoubtedly a distinctively human phenomenon that can only develop when a certain threshold of mimesis is transcended." Girard, *Things Hidden Since the Foundation of the World*, 283.

12. Psychological studies have confirmed the unconscious nature of mimetic desire. See, for instance, Garrels, *Mimesis and Science,* Kindle Location 758.

13. "Empirical researchers speak of imitation as the primary source of one's access and attachment to the mind and being of the other, and that these mimetic connections foster the opening of intersubjective experience to deeper and more penetrating levels of relationality and social cognition." Antonello, Pierpaolo and Gifford, Paul, *How We Became Human: Mimetic Theory and the Science of Evolutionary Origins.* (East Lansing: Michigan State University Press, Kindle Location 2507, 2015.)

makes possible for us the breakout from routinely animalistic appetites, and constructs our own, albeit inevitably unstable, identities."[14]

Similar to process philosophy, mimetic theory recognizes an intimate link between the complexity of human desire and identity. Jean-Michel Oughourlian goes as far to say: "there is no self apart from desire, that it is desire that animates the self, and that the self is a 'self-of-desire'."[15] Our reflective capacity also opens us up to the extremes of human experience, both positive and negative—something inevitable in our evolutionary progress. We should note here the significance of Girard's terminology of *openness* and *freedom*:

If desire were not mimetic, we would not be open to what is human and what is divine. Mimetic desire enables us to escape from the animal realm. It is responsible for the best and the worst in us, for what lowers us below the animal levels as well as what elevates us above it. Our unending discords are the ransom for our freedom.[16]

Mimetic desire opens us up to what is human and what is divine, for in relationship with others and with God, mimesis allows us to share in the very interiority of another. The mimetic sharing of desires can draw us toward common possibilities, toward the same goals, and in so doing strengthen the relationship. Instinctual

---

14. Girard, *Evolution and Conversion,* 42-43.

15. Jean-Michel Oughourlian and Eugene Webb, *The Genesis of Desire.* (East Lansing: Michigan State University Press, 2010), 33.

16. Girard, *I see Satan Fall like Lightning.* 16.

appetites keep animals bound to the limited behavior of their group.[17] But humans can mimetically receive desires beyond their immediate group and thereby develop new skills and move toward a new destination. Girard concludes: "Instead of being limited to instinctual patterns, we are capable of learning the most diverse lessons of culture. "[18]

Mimetic desire is structured in a specific way. According to Girard, desire doesn't just spontaneously erupt between a person and the object of desire, but relies on a mediator, a model, someone who the subject imitates. He envisions mimetic desire as triangular, consisting of the imitator (or subject), the model, and the object of desire.[19] The subject desires a given object *because* the mediator desires it.

Humans are social creatures, finding identity in a relational network, and constantly pursuing a greater sense of being. Girard also says we are prone to a sense of lack and often see in others what we sense we lack in ourselves. This creates an environment in which the desires of the model can easily be transferred mimetically. Girard identified this "lack of being" in his earlier works, as a central human characteristic.[20] The psychoanalyst, Jacques Lacan, also views a sense of lack in early childhood development as part of an inevitable

---

17. "If desire is only mine, I will always desire the same things. If desire is so fixed, it means that there isn't much difference between desire and instincts. In order to have mobility of desire—in relation to both appetites and instincts from one side and the social milieu from the other—the relevant difference is imitation, that is, the presence of the model or models, since everybody has one or more." (Girard, *Evolution and Conversion,* 42).

18. Girard, *Things Hidden since the Foundation of the World,* 85.

19. "The real third party is the subject himself, and if his desire always takes a triangular form, it is because it is the carbon copy of a pre-existing desire, his rival's desire." (Ibid. 339).

20. See René Girard, *Violence and the Sacred,* trans Patrick Gregory (Baltimore: John Hopkins University Press, 1977) and René Girard, *Deceit, Desire, and the Novel: Self and other in Literary Structure.* (The Johns Hopkins University Press, 2010).

process in the formation of self-consciousness.[21] We might see similarities with the Genesis 3 text, in which humans desire and grasp (at the suggestion of the mediating serpent) for the very fruit that promises greater "being."[22]

Mimetic Conflict

According to mimetic theory, the uniqueness of our human imitative capacities, coupled with the complexity of desire, enable both new dimensions of connection and intensities of conflict. As we saw in the previous section, the human *self* shouldn't be understood as an isolated subject but as formed in relationship with others—a self-of-desire. Sharing the same desires can easily lead to rivalry: if the model's object of desire cannot be shared, conflict will ensue, especially because our sense of identity unconsciously links to our desires. Girard shows how human conflict arises from mimetic desire and the new intensity of relationship it makes possible.

Many philosophers have spoken about imitation and desire, but Girard's thought connects all these pieces into an exceptionally coherent story of human development. He recognizes that some mimetic relationships likely won't result in conflict. For instance, imitating the desire of a model that's beyond reach, such as a celebrity, or a fictional character, seldom causes conflict. The objects of desire of these mediators are simply too vague or too unattainable. Girard calls this *external mediation,* when the mediator is on a different social plane and their objects of desire are just too far away

---

21. "A 'mirror stage' attests to a founding alienation, a lack of being." (Alison, *The Palgrave Handbook of Mimetic Theory and Religion*, 39).

22. For a Girardian reading of Genesis 3 see: Jean-Michel Oughourlian and Eugene Webb, *The Genesis of Desire.* (East Lansing: Michigan State University Press, 2010).

to compete over and possess.[23] However, when the model is a peer, the proximity makes conflict more likely. Girard names this second instance *internal mediation*.[24] In this instance, I desire to possess the same object the mediator desires. When it appears as if a peer is preventing me from attaining my desire (a desire I unconsciously appropriated from my peer), hostility naturally increases.

This produces a paradox: in such close proximity, the initial object of desire quickly becomes forgotten as the focus shifts to the model/obstacle that keeps me from my desire. The model mirrors back the subject's mimetic desire, increasing the rivalry. Each rival becomes obsessed with the other and both become imitators of the hostility they perceive in the other. Although the rivals see the other as different, and believe that these differences cause the conflict, the truth is that they fight because they are the same. Each one reaches for a fuller and more satisfying sense of being and perceives the other as the obstacle to such satisfaction. When one expects the worst in another, such suspicions are soon confirmed. Retaliatory blows give way to preemptive blows:

> Doubling occurs as soon as the object has disappeared in the heat of the rivalry: the two rivals become more and more concerned with defeating the opponent for the sake of it, rather than obtaining the object, which eventually becomes irrelevant, as it only exists as an excuse for the escalation of the dispute. Thus, the rivals become more and more undifferentiated, identical: doubles. A mimetic crisis is always a crisis of undifferentiation that erupts when the roles of

---

23. Girard, *Evolution and Conversion*, 42.
24. Ibid.

subject and model are reduced to that of rivals. It's the disappearance of the object which makes it possible.[25]

This whole process reveals that the awakening of desire connects not simply to the object of desire, but to the fulness of being represented by the model.[26] This sense of lack-of-being is what unconsciously fuels rivalry. We perceive the rival as withholding what we desire. Genesis 3 has a similar perspective on the development of human consciousness, namely that the twisting of desire forms the basis for misunderstanding God and ourselves. This imagined god withholds what we think we lack. The felt lack within produces impatient grasping after the forbidden fruit.

This sense of lack (unique to the human sense of self) drives humans to fight more vehemently and do more barbaric things than animals. Animals engage in rivalry, but most animals will avoid physical damage in their rivalry. Typically, for instance, rivalry for a female animal will be resolved as soon as one of the animals demonstrates superior power. But humans may continue fighting until someone dies, for our sense of lack connects not directly to the nature of the object desired, but to an underlying sense of an insufficient self.

Harmonization Terms and Clarifications

I will seek next to describe Girard's concept of mimetic desire through Whiteheadian categories, to see what can be gained. When Girard

---

25. Ibid.

26. "Kristeva and Girard agree that human origins are shaped by imitation. According to Girard, mimetic desire arises in humans because we lack being. Looking at another to inform us of what we should desire, each of us finds our attention drawn toward the object that the other recommends. But ultimately the object is only an indirect means of drawing nearer the other, whose apparent plentitude of being we wish to acquire." (Alison, *The Palgrave Handbook of Mimetic Theory and Religion*, 39).

speaks of a person, be that the subject or the model, we are referring to an identity that could span multiple Whiteheadian "occasions." Similarly, *desire* could span multiple occasions. As we have seen, according to Whitehead, appetition (or desire) serves as a guiding influence prevalent in every process of prehension. The sketch below will demonstrate that desire can be viewed as a complex instantiation of appetition and become the actual value (or what Whitehead calls the datum) prehended.

Using Whitehead's concept of the "actual occasion" as an analytical tool means there are various ways in which the process of mimetic desire can be arrested and atomized. We have previously established that we can use two perspectives to analyze a process, namely coordinate and genetic analysis. From a coordinate perspective, we seek to identify a definite fact, a realized value. In this instance, the process of mimetic desire produces the realized fact of a person desiring something. From a genetic perspective, we seek to identify the processes that produce this fact. Therefore, we will consider the episode in a person's life in which the desire forms to be the actual entity and subsequently, virtually divide the event utilizing prehensions. Hereafter in our discussion, I will use the terms "person," "actual occasion," and "actual entity" to refer to this episode or epoch within the person's life.

Girard describes the event of mimetic desire as a triangular movement involving the subject, the model, and the object of desire. Whitehead describes prehension as having a vector character involving emotion, purpose, value, and causation.[27] Above, we defined mimesis as an unconscious form of imitation that extends beyond external relations and which includes the unconscious process of

---

27. Whitehead, *Process and Reality*, 19.

perceiving and duplicating the interiority of another. Mimesis, however, does not necessarily imply an exact copy. Rather, it speaks of the unconscious transfer of a feeling. In the Whiteheadian schema, every prehension "consists of three factors: (a) the 'subject' which is prehending, namely, the actual entity in which that prehension is a concrete element; (b) the 'datum' which is prehended; (c) the 'subjective form' which is how that subject prehends that datum."[28]

If Girard's mimetic processes correspond to Whitehead's concept of prehensions on an ontological level, we should be able to use this same analytical description. Therefore, we can view the process of mimetic desire as:

(a) the episode within the person's life (subject or actual entity) in which that mimetic relationship (prehension) is a concrete element;

(b) the desire (the datum, or actual content) which is mimetically reflected (prehended); and

(c) the 'subjective form' as how the person contextualizes and interprets (prehends) that desire (datum).

Put simply, we'll be looking at that period in a person's life in which a mimetic desire formed, the relationships that formed the desire, and the subjective processes that might have shaped the desire. Girard does not develop his thoughts around (c) - - the interpretation and contextualization of the desire. His emphasis remains on the imitation (a and b) of desire. He neglects, but does not explicitly exclude, the process of interpretation. Here Whiteheadian insights could be enriching to Girardian discourse.

---

28. Ibid., 23.

Analysis of Mimetic Desire

For Girard, all desire is desire for being, meaning that the subject perceives the immediate experience of self as less than what it could be. Metaphysically, to put it in Whitehead's terms, the actual entity prehends a previous occurrence of itself which emphasizes the fact that what it was, and what it is, is less than what it could be. This prehension of a previous instance is in the process of being harmonized with conceptual prehensions, that is, possibilities. For Girard, this sense of lack originates the process of mimetic desire. For Whitehead, the possibility of greater satisfaction as a unified self (being) awakens appetition in entities. He writes: "Appetition is immediate matter of fact including in itself a principle of unrest, involving realization of what is not and may be."[29] The tension created between what is actual and what is possible is the energy that animates the occasion. Appetition becomes an internal drive toward more intense, diverse, and complex experiences, thereby increasing/ reaching satisfaction. Whitehead continues: "In its self-creation the actual entity is guided by its ideal of itself as individual satisfaction and as transcendent creator."[30]

Both Whiteheadian appetition and Girardian desire emerge in the space between what is and what could be; they can be understood as the tension created by the contrast between the actual and the possible. We can describe both as an urge to transcend the current self. Possibilities of an ideal version of the self, contrast with the previous occasion of self and are now seeking to be included in this creative process. So far, we have prehensions of the previous occasion of self that affirms a sense of lack, and prehensions of possibilities of

---

29. Ibid., 32.
30. Ibid., 85.

greater "being" or an ideal version of self. Desire is how we feel the future or how we feel possibility. In other words, desire is how an entity envisions possibilities to be part of its future actuality.

Another prehension is in process, which is vital to Girard's understanding. It is the relationship between the subject (the actual entity) and a model. Within the context of the human psyche shaped by its social environment, this difference between what is and what could be, could easily give birth to a sense of existential lack-of-being. Instead of focusing on the possibilities of being that are open to us, we would then focus on the insufficiency of the current self. Consequently, we tend to perceive in others what we sense we lack in ourselves. The possibilities of an ideal self find their concrete representation in the model.

However, attempting to apprehend the substance of a model proves to be complicated. What the subject prehends is, in fact, the model's desire, which is the most substantial aspect of the human self. However, here we locate where misinterpretation can take place and desire become twisted. The subject's desire for fulness of being is deflected to the model's object of desire, which can never satisfy the underlying desire. All of this happens unconsciously. Consciously, a person might simply realize that they desire something specific. However, where this desire comes from is not easily recognized. We often perceive desires as originating within ourselves. However, in reality the self doesn't just *have* desires, it's formed by desire; both Girard and Whitehead recognize that desire is formative of self.

The formation of a mimetic desire need not necessarily spark the beginning of conflict, even though that tends to be Girard's focus. The creation of a mimetic desire could be a positive development that gives direction and brings fulfillment to a person. For instance, a person might recognize qualities such as courage or kindness in a model. To be inspired to be kind and courageous is unlikely to cause conflict with the model. We will discuss this type of possibility in more detail in the next chapter.

Intensification of Appetition into Mimetic Desire

Whitehead's concept of appetition applies not only to humans but to all creative processes. Girard draws a distinction between appetites and desire, specifically to highlight the complex psychological movements within mimetic desire.[31] The correlations I draw don't nullify this distinction but exemplify it. I propose that what distinguishes Girardian desire from Whiteheadian appetite is the intensity and complexity of the psychological process. Girard's concept of mimetic desire is a complex and uniquely human instantiation of appetition. Whitehead recognized that the complexity of human consciousness reshapes appetition:

> In physical experience, the forms are the defining factors; in mental experience the forms connect the immediate occasions with occasions that lie beyond. The connection of immediate fact with the future resides in its appetitions. The higher forms of intellectual experience only arise when there are complex integrations, and re-integrations, of mental and physical experience. Reason then appears as a criticism of appetitions. It is a second-order type of mentality. It is the appetitions of appetitions.[32]

---

31. Girard, *Evolution and Conversion*, 41.

32. Whitehead, Alfred. N. *The Function of Reason*. (Baltimore: Agora Publications. Kindle Edition. 2014). Location 361.

Let's go back to our thought experiment. The episode we are considering seeks to describe the creation of a mimetic desire in which we have precisely the kind of complex integration Whitehead speaks of. We can see at least two forms of appetition operating here: first, the appetition that guides the process of prehension toward satisfaction, and second, the prehended desire itself. Using Whitehead's terminology, the first appetition is satisfied within the boundaries of the actual occasion. Its satisfaction is the creation of a desire. But the second complex desire isn't satisfied within the boundaries of this occasion. Rather it becomes part of an enduring identity that spans multiple occasions. We can interpret Whitehead's "appetitions of appetitions" as both a complexification and an intensification of desire. Whitehead's statement that reason "appears as a criticism of appetitions" has striking correlations with Girard's ideas of the emergence of symbolic thought, something I will explore later.

According to Girard, mimetic desire increases our capacity for both good and evil. To review,

> If desire were not mimetic, we would not be open to what is human and what is divine. Mimetic desire enables us to escape from the animal realm. It is responsible for the best and the worst in us, for what lowers us below the animal levels as well as what elevates us above it. Our unending discords are the ransom for our freedom.[33]

We can see the theme of increased capacity and intensity of experience in both the concepts of appetition and mimetic desire.

---

33. Girard, *I see Satan fall like lightning*, 16.

Despite using distinct terminology, they are both observing the same ontological process—the same reality.

For Whitehead, every occasion has a formative aim (a teleological lure) and the relevant possibilities necessary for a unique self, which constitutes a primordial fact—God, in Whitehead's language. Some possibilities are more attractive (desirable) than others within the creative event of becoming. Desire opens us up and connects us more intimately with specific relationships and possibilities. Appetition/desire, by its very definition, disrupts indifference and intensifies preference. Whitehead recognizes God's unique role in awakening our desire for beauty.

Girard does not often use God-language when describing the formation of desire, but that doesn't make these perspectives incompatible. Taking into account that for Whitehead, "God" represents not a separate entity but a process that is operative in all processes, it would be consistent with—even necessary—that the initial aim that shapes an occasion would come through the process of prehending other occasions. One might argue that the initial aim comes logically prior to the prehensions. However, there is no reason why the initial aim could not be a more general desire, which is subsequently defined more clearly by the prehensions. Girard's insistence that desire begins outside the person remains consistent with Whitehead's view that we are lured toward a beauty larger than our immediate selves.

When Girard asserts that mimetic desire opens us to what is human and to what is divine, I recognize in that statement a harmonization with Whitehead's idea of a divine lure. Girard recognizes the creative role of mimetic desire and the beautiful possibilities it opens in relationship with others and with God, but in his work as a whole does not develop the concept of this creative side. But although Girard focuses on the conflictual aspects of mimetic desire and the many perils into which this increased capacity has led humanity, I would argue that the overall aim of this capacity and the trajectory of the Girardian narrative moves toward a greater degree of freedom—"Our unending discords are the ransom of our freedom."[34] Although it is not always obvious in his work, at least here we can see that Girard recognized a positive trajectory in mimetic processes. In fact, Girard states that "mimetic desire is inherently good," that is, in its ultimately creative capacity.[35] This creative mimetic trajectory correlates with the Whiteheadian concept of a divine lure towards beauty. For Whitehead, freedom is an essential part of beauty.

Mimetic desire represents both a continuity of the more general concept of appetition and a radical discontinuity from its animal instantiations. The Neurobiologist, William B. Hurlbut, who engages mimetic theory in his work, also recognizes the broader principle of desire, writes:

The emotions, which have their evolutionary origin in physiological regulation of basic body processes such as circulation, posture, and readiness of response, are drawn more deeply into the inward intensity of wider intentions, empowering persistence toward more distant goals. As the philosopher Hans Jonas explains, "Animal being is thus essentially passionate being" (Jonas 1966, 106). And passion

---

34. Ibid.

35. Girard makes this statement in a 1993 interview with Rebecca Adams. See "The Goodness of Mimetic Desire," in *The Girard Reader*, ed. James Williams (New York: Crossroad, 1996), 62-65. This is an excerpt of a longer interview; see Girard, Rene. "Violence Difference Sacrifice: A Conversation with Rene Girard," interviewed by Rebecca J. Adams. *Religion and Literature* 25, no. 2 (Summer 1993), 9-33.

motivates and sustains effortful action toward broader and more distant horizons of need. Lifted beyond the immediacy of fundamental physical and chemical conditions, life extends its reach and realm. Jonas continues, "Fulfillment not yet at hand is the essential condition of desire, and deferred fulfillment is what desire in turn makes possible" (Jonas 1966, 101). In all of these ways, desire, as a primal principle of being, extends the scope of life, magnifying its freedom, intensity, and inward sense of meaning.[36]

Hurlbut's insights are equally relevant to process philosophy and mimetic theory. The themes of self-transcendence, intensification of experience, freedom, and desire run through both. I would argue that Girard's concept of mimetic desire is indeed a complex, intensified, and uniquely human instantiation of Whiteheadian appetition.

Analysis of Mimetic Conflict

The event of mimetic conflict can also be analyzed as an actual occasion. Girard helps us understand that conflict arises most often as the result of frustrated desire. Furthermore, desire becomes frustrated because someone stands in the way, or becomes an obstacle, between the subject and the object of desire. For Girard, the obstacle is most often the model because they share a desire for the same object, through the subject's imitation of the model's desire. And when two hands reach for the same object, conflict frequently happens. This can be an uncomfortable truth, for it reveals that the one I am in conflict with is also a model for me on an unconscious level.

---

36. Antonello, *How We Became Human*, Kindle Location 2898.

To return to our analysis, now looking at the second instance, in which we have what Whitehead calls appetition of appetition. Let us say the episode or epoch we will identify constitutes the period in the person's life where frustration arises and conflict results. We'll keep the same actors as in the previous episode in which we saw how mimetic desire comes about. However, the occasion is new. In this occasion, the subject inherits (prehends) the desire from the previous occasion, a previous instance of self. Consequently, the link to the model becomes vague and the illusion that the desire originates in self becomes intensified. Let's look at how the subject misinterprets this. Underlying the subject's desire is the conceptual valuation (and misinterpretation) that a new sense of fulness will be achieved in attaining the object of desire. The object of desire takes on a significance far beyond an external object as its attainment is now linked to the person's sense of self. Note however, that though this is a misinterpretation, it does not make the feeling less real.

Suppose the subject and the model both act to attain the object, two hands both reaching for the same thing. One of the actors in this scenario will likely deprive the other of attaining the object, with conflict erupting. This conflict will be likely to escalate far beyond what is reasonable, for unconsciously the value and very existence of self is at stake. But as the subject imitates the model, the person doesn't recognize the origin of their desire in the other, nor the misinterpretation that has joined the object of desire to their sense of self-worth.

So far, we have focused on the scene of conflict between subject and model, the scenario that Girard tends to stress. Combining Whiteheadian and Girardian concepts of desire, however, creates a richer insight into the process and helps us construct a creative model of desire. And it's to that construction of co-creative desire we turn in the next chapter.

5

Co-Creative Desire

We now turn our attention to how combining Whitehead and Girard's understanding of desire, as done in the previous chapter, can help us construct a creative model of desire. As mentioned before, Girard chose the word *mimesis* rather than imitation because he wanted to emphasize the unconscious nature of the process.[1] This unconscious aspect, this lack of awareness, begins in the formation of desire, continues in conflictual relationships, and proves essential for the scapegoating process to work effectively.[2] "To scapegoat someone," Girard remarks, "is to be unaware of what you are doing."[3]

In our ancient origin myths, we find a conscious attempt to describe the events that were driven by these unconscious processes, but this results in a fundamental misinterpretation that manifests as blind spots in our myths. Girard uses the term *conversion* to describe the process that exposes our misinterpretations. Conversion can be

---

1. "There is less awareness in mimetism and more in imitation." (Girard, *Evolution and Conversion*, 44).

2. "Moreover, there is always a blind spot in our perception of reciprocal hostility, competition and rivalry. We are ready to deconstruct anything except the idea that we are self-directed and that the persecutors are always the others." (Ibid., 8).

3. Ibid., 62.

understood as a revelation that makes us aware of what we were ignorant of, and which brings about a greater consciousness of the movements that shape our desires. As such, the death of Christ, according to Girard, is the moment that subverts our mythical misunderstandings most clearly because it exposes scapegoating for what it truly is.[4] Jesus' words on the cross: "Father forgive them for they know not what they are doing"[5] vividly illustrate this point about unconsciousness. In this moment of unveiling, we can see human actions were driven by motivations to which we were oblivious.

However, Girard did not apply this process of conversion to his concept of mimetic desire with the same rigor as he applied it to the concept of scapegoating. If mimetic desire is, by its very definition, reliant on the process being unconscious, then the form of that process will be transformed when it is brought into greater conscious awareness. Girard does recognize that something new happens in the person of Jesus and that we, too, can break free from the violent mimetic cycle.[6] However, exactly how and why the structure of desire changes is not clear in his work. I plan to show how the structure of desire changes as it is brought into conscious awareness.

I would reiterate that the process of desire, however, will never be fully conscious. Instead, we can find a new balance between the

---

4. "The Gospels become the hermeneutical key that allows us to rethink both mythology and ancient texts as the progressive coming-to-terms of humanity with the violent matrix of the cultural order. Christ's sacrifice is the moment of complete disclosure of the arbitrariness of the victimary mechanism on which the sacred and symbolic order of archaic societies was built and kept stable. In this sense, Girard goes against common assumptions, and takes on board the Judeo-Christian tradition." (Ibid., 9.)

5. Luke 23:34.

6. "…but the individual isn't bound hand-and-foot to mimetic desire. Jesus himself was not. To talk about freedom means to talk about man's ability to resist the mimetic mechanism. Hence, the only freedom we have is to imitate Jesus, that is, by not joining the mimetic cycle. Or to imitate someone like Jesus." (Girard, *Evolution and Conversion*, 159).

conscious and unconscious aspects of desire, exactly the type of environment that makes creativity possible. The structure of desire then becomes semi-mimetic and semi-conscious. Part of this new unveiling of the structure of desire is accepting that others are involved in forming my desire. I propose the terminology "co-creative desire" to describe this synergetic and collaborative type of desire.

We will begin by examining the most basic Girardian assumption regarding the formation of desire. For Girard, models transform into rivals through acquisitive mimetic desire because of a foundational sense of lack-of-being. By providing a different foundation for the awakening of desire, or at least a more nuanced understanding of it, we lay the foundation for transforming the structure of mimetic desire.

In a cosmos drawn forward by beauty and goodness, there will be a natural advance in human development from force to persuasion, according to Whitehead.[7] We can add to this by saying that if indeed we have a God of love luring the world forward, we can also expect a progression from indifference to love and from self-preservation to self-giving. As humanity becomes more conscious of the processes that undergird it, we can expect that the human obsession with being and actualization through grasping or attempting to possess some substance will be tempered with an appreciation for *becoming* itself. Or stated another way, our definition of *being* needs to acknowledge the significance of the relationships and processes that shape our being. I've identified three areas in which we can make the movements of desire more conscious, thereby transforming the structure of desire into a more creative movement.

---

7. Whitehead, Alfred. N. Chapter V. "From Force to Persuasion." In *Adventures of Ideas*. (New York: Free Press, 2010).

1. From Lack-of-being to Possibilities-of-being

We've described the Girardian sense of lack-of-being as the tension between what is and what could be. Within the human psyche, this sense of lack is uniquely linked to our relationships with others. However, this sense of lack doesn't always have to develop into an existential crisis that transforms others into rivals. One of the ways we can introduce a more nuanced understanding of this sense of lack-of-being would be by examining where the focus falls in this tension between what is and what could be.

Let's begin with a hypothetical example: young children might be perfectly content with playing in a sandpit, yet if asked if they want to go to the beach, a new desire might be awakened by this new possibility. Then if some of the children got to go to the beach and others were kept behind in the sandpit, the tension would increase.

Let's take this step by step. Beginning with all the children in the sandpit, the possibility of going to the beach could awaken a new desire simply because the children are now comparing two situations. The tension between what is, and what could be, can be experienced as a sense of lack in the present situation, but probably not as a sense of *existential* lack-of-being. If the focus shifts onto the future possibility, then the experience would simply be excitement about new possibilities, rather than an overwhelming sense of insufficiency. I am happy to admit that this tension probably always includes a bit of both—an awareness of the present and a drawing toward a better future. However, where we place most of our focus will determine whether a perceived lack of the present, or the promise of an abundant future, serves as the greater motivator. Remember, Whitehead identifies three aspects to a prehension and the third is the *subjective form*. The subjective form is the way in which the situation is interpreted. How future possibilities become reconciled with present realities is not a determined process but a creative interpretation.

When the situation progresses, and some kids are selected to go to the beach, the tension becomes more complex, for now we have not simply a comparison between two situations but between a "self" and an "other" like me. This triangular-relational dimension to desire is far more likely to give rise to a feeling of lack-of-being and shift the focus from the object/situation desired onto the being of the other—the *other* that seems to have what *self* lacks. A disproportionate focus on the present lack, combined with a comparison to others, will develop into a sense of lack-of-being and distort one's vision of others as models that seem to contain a fullness of being.

I want to develop this thought further by applying this shift-in-focus principle, thereby defining two types of lack. The first type of lack refers to a sense of insufficiency based on my present state compared to others. Girard most often refers to this type of lack in describing twisted mimetic desire. The second type of lack simply represents the difference between the present and the future and might not involve a sense of insufficiency at all, nor a comparison to others. The fact that the present does not contain the fulness of actuality, but continues to actualize possibilities, can logically be interpreted as a form of lack. With this distinction it becomes possible to simultaneously be content with my present self and excited about future possibilities—a logical type of lack. This distinction will also become significant when we consider how desire and lack applies to God.

In summary, we can posit a sliding scale in the tension between the present lack and the future possibility, influenced by where we place the focus. We have the creative freedom to interpret the situation in such a way that it energizes us to reach for new possibilities, or we can interpret the tension as a judgment on our present state of lack. Because we are social creatures, this tension takes on a complex structure. In the following section, we will look at how a process perspective of possibilities provides a solid foundation for this shift in focus.

2. Relocating the Possibilities-of-being

From a Whiteheadian process perspective, desire is awakened by possibilities of beauty that promise greater intensities and satis-faction of experience. In this generalized description of desire, we have no need for a human model. God is the source of this vision of beauty. Understandably, some may protest that Whitehead's de-scription of desire remains too abstract, especially within the human context. But Whitehead allows for the idea to be brought into a more practical realm by noting that these divine possibilities are al-ways contextualized to the situation in which an entity finds itself.[8] Whitehead sees God working through the reality of our conditioned standpoint—the relationships we find ourselves in—and describes the process as follows: "He is the lure for feeling, the eternal urge of desire. His particular relevance to each creative act, as it arises from its own conditioned standpoint in the world, constitutes him the initial 'object of desire' establishing the initial phase of each subjec-tive aim."[9] Consequently, part of the contextualization of possibil-ities comes through the awakening of desire by means of the models with whom we are in relationship.

---

8. Whitehead sees the process of bringing pure potentials and actual entities together and ad-justing desires accordingly, as the very definition of *relevance* and a function of the primordial nature of God. See Whitehead, *Process and Reality*, 32.

9. Whitehead, *Process and Reality*, 344.

Combining Girardian and Whiteheadian perspectives of desire opens an important insight into the nature of the model. We could look at it this way: the model does not contain the fullness of being I lack, but instead plays a role in contextualizing and communicating divine possibilities of being. As such, one can honor the model as an inspiring exemplar and enabler of a fuller being without any need to possess the model's being. Exemplars are non-conflictual models. The qualities we find inspiring in them are transcendent values such as courage, kindness etc. Objects of desire are absent or vague in these relationships. Also, becoming more conscious that my desires always have a transcendent goal, namely a transcendent self, means that objects of desire become less significant. I think most spiritual leaders would agree that diminished desire for 'stuff'—material objects without a deeper relational meaning—is a good thing.

From a process perspective, the desirable possibilities of being always reside outside of any one entity, in the divine vision of beauty. Recognizing the model consciously as a mediator brings a healthy balance to the relationship, for it prevents me from forming an unhealthy attachment to one who supposedly possesses the fullness of being I desire. This recognition also makes it unlikely for rivalry to escalate dangerously in the mistaken belief that the rival has the power to give or take away my very being. This results in a more transparent and authentic model of desire, meaning that I'm more aware of the role others play in shaping my desires and simultaneously aware that the possibilities of a fuller being reside beyond these models, in the mind of God.

Authenticity is often associated with the absence of influences—and seen as the opposite of imitation. Such a view is deeply flawed because, according to both mimetic theory and process philosophy, the very nature of reality is relational. Authentic desire is therefore not found in the absence of influences but in the recognition of the influences that uniquely shape desire. Authenticity has more to do with the interpretive/creative process than the singularity of origin.

The Whiteheadian perspective of relationality can also enrich the Girardian concept of *interdividuality*. Girard recognized that an individual constitutes a dynamic movement formed by its relationships with others, hence the neologism "interdividual." As we have seen, desire energizes relational movements. Whitehead agrees but extends the idea of subjective relationship as a characteristic of *all* entities. Every relationship therefore becomes an opportunity, a contextualized possibility, to move closer to the divine vision of beauty. The *telos*, the ultimate aim of my being, will never therefore be located in any one relationship. Yet every relationship can be valued because it contains contextualized possibilities for greater beauty. This includes relationships with other humans but also with other non-human entities and processes.

Becoming more aware of where the possibilities of being arise, greatly influences our relationships with others, including those defined as models. Locating possibilities of being beyond any one model makes it more likely that our relationships with models will be healthy: neither over-attached nor dangerously rivalrous. A greater consciousness of this process of desire will likely reduce superficial desire for objects and enhance our desire for more meaningful relationships. Combining the insights of Girard and Whitehead makes the process of desire more transparent and, as such, allows us to participate in the process more consciously. The result is more authentic desire as one acknowledges the influences, recognizes the underlying source of possibilities, and applies creative interpretations.

3. Redefining Being

We began exploring the role others play in the formation of self in the previous section. From a process perspective, "being" shouldn't be understood as a static possession; neither is it limited to my present condition. Rather, the possibilities of being open to me already constitute part of the dynamic that forms me in this moment.

The philosopher Jean-Luc Marion sheds further light on this theme and the human pursuit of being.[10] He begins his argument by showing that the being we seek will not be found in the measure of actuality but in possibility.[11] Marion's observation has obvious correlations with Whitehead's categories of actuality and possibility. In other words, simply knowing that I exist has little value. But what intrigues me and makes me come alive are the possibilities of being, which are open to me.

Marion develops his argument further by showing how certainty in my own existence is vanity, for it has a circular reference in which I assure myself. However, I need not self-certainty but an assurance that comes from elsewhere. For such an assurance that comes from elsewhere gives me a foundation that is more secure than my own mere vanity or self-certainty. From a Girardian perspective, this need for an assurance coming from elsewhere would partly explain why models emerge so naturally. Marion continues to show that this assurance, though, has to assure me of something more than my own existence—for we have already seen that the measure of my being won't be found in actuality. What's the use of simply existing? It has to assure me of my possibility, and a specific possibility in particular: that I am loved.

---

10. Jean-Luc Marion and Stephen E. Lewis, *The Erotic Phenomenon.* (Chicago: The University of Chicago Press, 2008).

11. Ibid., 11-37.

Finally, Marion asks if this love can only be reciprocal or whether, in some way, I can find the initiative to love; whether there might be a love that "issues from deep within an elsewhere that is more inward to me than me myself, preceded or validated by no assurance at all." Such a love gives no assurance of being. In fact, it completely subverts the pursuit of being as a substance to possess. For this love is an act of giving or losing your being and it thereby overcomes the fear of loss. "Loving surpasses being with an excess that has no measure."[12]

In the act of love, the pursuit of being becomes irrelevant. Love is therefore the antithesis of the pursuit of being (as a possession). This love does so much more than affirm my being; it continually draws me beyond the certainty of actuality into the future of possibility and transforms me into one be-loved. Marion writes: "For I could not be, nor accept to endure in being, without at least the open possibility that at one moment or another someone is loving me. For me, to be, signifies nothing less than to be-loved."[13]

Girard helped us see how the movements of desire shape our sense of self. Whitehead shows that the continual flow of reality is a fundamental characteristic of being. Marion's argument touches on the misunderstandings present in our pursuit of being and offers an alternative way of being, namely, to be-loved. Being be-loved means to find my existence in a source of love beyond myself. The possibility to love and be loved totally redefines my sense of self for this possibility does not reside in any one model, and not even in my current self, but in "an elsewhere that is more inward to me than me myself."[14]

---

12. Ibid.

13. Ibid., 21.

14. Ibid.

Another contemporary philosopher who argues for a creative vision of mimetic desire is Robin Collins. In an essay entitled "Nature as a Source of Non-Conflictual Desire," he begins a creative Girardian analysis by surveying religious and philosophical intuitions about the nature of being and desire.[15] He concludes the survey by noting that the "mystical idea of nature as a deep, unified, creative whole not only appears throughout the traditions discussed in this section, but as argued later, is suggested by major developments in twentieth-century science."[16] He then continues to develop his definition of persons as distinct "loci of interbeing" whose "telos is to reflect, internalize, and appropriately interrelate with the reality of other beings."[17] He names this interrelation with others, *interbeing*, a term borrowed from the Buddhist teacher Thich Nhat Hanh. Regarding the way in which our awareness of interbeing can influence the nature of desire, he concludes:

> Insofar as we come to truly recognize that our own being is constituted by our interbeing with others (including nature), we will come to recognize that the more they gain in fullness of reality, the more we enrich ourselves by internalizing their reality and their interconnectedness with us.[18]

The Girardian scholar Rebecca Adams clarifies how mimetic desire can be creative and further constructs a model of generative interdividuality or interbeing. Girard recognized her insights as an

---

15. Ryba. *René Girard and Creative Mimesis*, 289.

16. Ibid., 290.

17. Ibid., 291.

18. Ibid., 297.

extension of his own thought.[19] Adams shows that twisted mimetic desire always involves some form of objectification. The object then becomes the location or opportunity for conflict. However, Adams demonstrates how desiring the subjectivity of another as the "object" within the mimetic triangle transforms the very meaning of an object and enriches both the self *and* the other. Adams's model of mimetic desire as love precludes objectification of either the one desiring or the one desired. This suggestion beautifully flows together with Whitehead's ontological insights, for to objectify anything, from a Whiteheadian perspective, is to miss its internal value and actual meaning.

I conclude that redefining being by introducing the transcendent quality of love brings a balance to our relationship with others and opens new creative possibilities. For my being will not be made fuller by possessing what others have or possessing what others are, but by the act of love, in the process of becoming.

The Scriptures and Co-creative Desire

Let's look at how all we have said overlaps with theology and statements found in the New Testament. These ideas are not explicitly Girard's or Whitehead's, but rather my own harmonization of co-creative desire with the biblical texts.

The Apostle Paul also recognized the danger inherent in social comparisons: "*For we dare not class ourselves or compare ourselves with those who commend themselves. But they, measuring themselves by themselves, and comparing themselves among themselves, are not wise.*" (2 Corinthians 10:12.) The form desire takes and the consequences

---

19. See Adams, Rebecca J. "Loving Mimesis and Girard's 'Scapegoat of the Text'": A Creative Reassessment of Mimetic Desire." In *Violence Renounced: Rene Girard, Biblical Studies and Peacemaking*, ed. Willard M. Swartley (Telford, PA: Pandora Press, 2000): 277-307.

it produces will be greatly influenced by the environment which nurtures it, whether an environment of lack and fear or an environment of excitement and wonder.

As we've noted before, these processes of comparing ourselves to others and reflecting their desires mostly happen on an unconscious level. If we bring these unconscious processes into conscious awareness, however, we can transform the dysfunctional and potentially harmful aspects of mimetic desire into something more beneficial. If we become aware that the very nature of reality is a process of becoming, that there is no stable or static *being* to possess, then we can shift the focus from a sense of the present lack onto the process and the possibilities it opens.

Instead of grasping after being, we could participate in a new awareness of the unending flow toward beauty, which nurtures a self-giving attitude—an attitude that was demonstrated by Christ Jesus: "*Have this mind among yourselves, which is yours in Christ Jesus, who, though he was in the form of God, did not count equality with God a thing to be grasped, but emptied himself*" (Philippians 2:5-7.) Such an attitude shift, however, would represent a radical shift in our understanding of identity or sense-of-being. An identity based on a sense of fullness allows Jesus to empty himself. Jesus demonstrates that a sense of fulness-of-being can replace a sense of lack-of-being. John 13 beautifully illustrates this:

> ...when Jesus knew that his hour had come to depart out of this world to the Father, having loved his own who were in the world, he loved them to the end. And during supper, when the devil had already put it into the heart of Judas Iscariot, Simon's son, to betray him, Jesus, knowing that the Father had given all things into his hands, and that he had

come from God and was going to God, rose from supper, laid aside his garments, and girded himself with a towel.

Most gospel texts tell us what Jesus said and did, but the text above seems to enter his mind and inform us about what he knew. For a moment here we're invited into the consciousness of Jesus—*knowing that the Father had given all things into his hands, and that he had come from God and was going to God.* It is this awareness of coming and going (as opposed to static being) and the fullness of possibilities placed within his hands—*the Father had given all things into his hands*—that gives Jesus the capacity to humble himself and serve. Love takes us beyond an obsession with being and a fear of non-being.

The author of Colossians recognized this same sense of fulness in Christ, writing: "*For in him the whole fulness of deity dwells bodily, and you have come to fulness of life in him*" (Colossians 2:9). The person of Christ and the message of the New Testament offers us a whole new basis for desiring and for constructing an identity no longer held hostage by a sense of lack, but liberated to give itself in the awareness of the overwhelming fullness of divine presence in this bodily form.

One might raise an objection here. If desire emerges in the space between what is and what could be, this still implies a difference between the present and the future in which the present is somehow less or lacking compared to the future. Otherwise, why would the future be desirable? Let's think about how this might apply to God, for instance. The idea that God lacks in any way would be inconceivable for many traditions. But here again, Whitehead helps us make helpful distinctions. What he calls God's *consequent* nature represents those aspects of God that are intertwined in relationship and affected by our temporal world. And in that context, God does indeed have a future, meaning that God is in process as well. The distinction we made earlier between the kind of lack that gives rise to a sense of insufficiency, and the logical lack that defines the difference between the present and the future, is significant when thinking about God's relationship to the future and to desire. God can participate in this second type of "lack" or openness to possibility and still be God.

To see this, consider the following. If we understand God as truly involved in our temporal world, we can confidently say that not all future possibilities are actualized for God. In this sense God logically lacks the actualization of future possibilities. However, simultaneously God has no sense of insufficiency or need to compare Godself with others. With this distinction between the two types of lack we can see the possibility of being satisfied with the present, yet excited about the future—of being content, yet desiring.

We have to use our imaginations as we apply these ideas to God. Why would an entity who is complete and whole desire anything... except to give itself? Can you imagine a wholeness so whole that the only way in which it could find novelty would be through fragmentation? A fulness so full that its only authentic expression would be in self-emptying? A completeness so complete that it could only progress by beginning anew? A consciousness so all-encompassing, so omnipresent that it would have to encapsulate parts of itself to produce unique perspectives? Such a complete, full, and whole consciousness would still have space for desire if love were its essence, for love cannot be obsessed with itself alone. Such a divine wholeness could still desire to give itself into many self-conscious units in order to create a diversity of beauty from embodied perspectives. This is exactly the kind of God we meet in the person of Jesus Christ.

Elizabeth Kraus articulates a similar vision of the divine in which we, and everything in the cosmos, can partake:

> Beauty diffuses itself, not through acts of efficient creation but through its infinite evocation of novel instances of itself: universes of creatures stirred by the creativity to become God-like by temporalizing the eternal togetherness of primordially ordered form in their concrete immediacy; universes of self-creating creatures whose response to the divine seduction is the incarnation of beauty.[20]

Jesus demonstrated how being human can be a novel instance of divine beauty. We can see here that the tension created between actuality and possibility does not necessarily have to be a negative lack-based, energy at all. Rather, the actual and what it contains (and does not contain) can be viewed as a positive value that contributes to the process of becoming. Psychologically, a person can be both content with what is, and also excited about what may be.

In summary, Girard's mimetic theory can and should be extended by developing a creative understanding of mimetic desire. As we've seen, some of the work has been done already, but much can still be done.[21] Such an extension will enrich its theological contribution and transformative effect. Girard's understanding of the gospel texts focuses on the exposure of the scapegoating process and its foundational role in forming religion and civilization.

---

20. Kraus, *The Metaphysics of Experience*, 224.

21. The implications of mimetic theory applied to atonement theology have been explored by several theologians. See Kirwan, *Mimesis and Atonement: René Girard and the Doctrine of Salvation*; and Robin Collins, "Girard and Atonement: An Incarnation Theory of Mimetic Participation," in *Violence Renounced: Rene Girard, Biblical Studies and Peacemaking* (Telford, PA: Pandora Press, 2000), 133-153.

He wants to show that the gospel revelation has a logic and unveils an anthropological truth that any rational person should be able to acknowledge without a faith commitment: "The Cross has indeed transformed the world, and we can interpret its power in a way that does not have to appeal to religious faith. We can give the triumph of the Cross a plausible meaning in a completely rational frame of reference."[22] This emphasis is very important, but incomplete as a representation of the gospel message.

In his later work, *Battling to the End,* Girard ponders the possibility that the revelation has failed, for it has not been heard.[23] Indeed, it seems something more than an objective anthropological revelation is needed. For Girard, unveiling the scapegoat mechanism is an act of negative revelation followed by the implied positive insight that God is not to be identified as the violent God of scapegoating. (For Girard, the resurrection of Jesus in the gospel narratives further testifies positively that God redeems the scapegoat, and has become the scapegoat to end scapegoating once and for all). This much we can get to anthropologically, that is, by simply reading the text. But Girard admits the message has apparently failed. But why? I would say because as we have seen, the scapegoating process and the subsequent development of religion and culture are dependent on a more foundational process, that of mimetic desire. Unless our Girardian understanding of the foundational process of mimetic desire can be transformed into a positive and creative movement, there's no basis for the subsequent processes to be transformed, even if they are exposed. This is the source of Girard's later pessimism—he is missing something important. Part of the gospel message is that

---

22. Girard, *I See Satan Fall Like Lightning*, 141.

23. Girard, René, and Benoît Chantre. *Battling to the End: Conversations with Benoît Chantre.* (East Lansing: Michigan State University Press, 2010), 46.

personal transformation is possible. Girard simply does not really develop how this is possible right now. But in both Girardian and Whiteheadian understanding, desire/appetition is a foundational aspect of identity. So we have to reconsider mimetic desire itself.

Girard comes closest to developing a positive understanding of mimetic desire in his exposition of John 8. Let's start with the actual text:

> **42** Jesus said to them, "If God were your Father, you would love Me, for I proceeded forth and came from God; nor have I come of Myself, but He sent Me. **43** Why do you not understand My speech? Because you are not able to listen to My word. **44** You are of *your* father the devil, and the desires of your father you want to do. He was a murderer from the beginning, and does not stand in the truth, because there is no truth in him. When he speaks a lie, he speaks from his own *resources,* for he is a liar and the father of it. (John 8:42-44)

Girard recognizes that we can choose between the extreme models—God or the devil —as the source of our desires: "The desire of which Jesus speaks is therefore based on imitation, whether of the devil or of God."[24] For him, God represents the kind of models who never become rivals "because they desire nothing in a greedy and competitive way." And so Girard concludes: "If the models that humans choose do not orient them in the right direction, one without conflict through Christ as intermediary, they expose themselves

---

24. Girard, *I See Satan Fall Like Lightning,* 39.

eventually to violent loss of differences and identity and thus to the single victim mechanism."[25]

Girard, therefore, acknowledges that a non-conflictual positive mimetic desire exists and that Christ somehow makes creative mimetic relationships possible. He has just not spelled out how this works. Here we find an opportunity to take mimetic theory beyond a general anthropologic revelation and apply it in a personal and psychological way.

The gospel message entails not only a revelation of the scapegoating process that exposes the structures of religion and culture, but a revelation of the structures of self. It exposes not only the misinterpretations of society, but my personal misinterpretations in the process of self-formation. Mimetic theory helps us diagnose the problem as both social and internal. When we do not creatively deal with the chaos within, when we hastily blame others rather than patiently transform, then we project our turmoil. It becomes a monstrous other, and so we contribute to this "satanic" cycle of accusation and violence. John chapter 8 is an example of how Jesus reinterprets the *satanic* as the cycle of accusation that leads to violence. The story is also an invitation to find a radically different model in the God who loves. We can rationally acknowledge the anthropological revelation in the scriptures without a faith commitment, but we cannot choose love as our model without being transformed by the creative desires that flow from this source.

This understanding of mimetic theory and co-creative desire can uniquely contribute to atonement theology. Following John 8 and the exploration of mimetic desire, John 9 develops the narrative further with the story of a man born blind. Jesus came to heal

---

25. Ibid.

humanity of a blindness we were *born with*—as Girardian theologian James Alison stresses, the enormity of our error only becomes evident post enlightenment. A man born blind has no memory of what it was like to see. The extent to which he cannot function normally, the extent of his blindness, will only be fully known after being healed. Experiencing restored sight allows him to fully realize what it meant to be blind! In this context, Jesus comes as the true light that enlightens every man (John 1:9) "to give us understanding, that we may know the true One, and we are in him who is true" (1 John 5:20). Jesus is the living demonstration of who God is, and therefore who we authentically are as being created in God's image and likeness.

As we've established, the most fundamental, rudimentary identity is the self-of-desire. When we lose sight of God's desire for us (the lure towards beauty in Whiteheadian language), when God's love is not the source of our reflection, then we are no longer truly ourselves. A mediated encounter with our projections and misinterpretations of God replaces a direct encounter with God. Consequently, Jesus comes to correct the most basic fault—no one has seen the Father, so no one has their true model in sight. So Jesus changes this by making the ideal model visible. "No one has seen God at any time. The only begotten Son, who is in the bosom of the Father, He has declared *Him*." (John 1:18)

Encountering Jesus in this mimetic/reflective way, transforms us (2 Corinthians 3:18) as we see again the authentic desire that gave us birth. The misinterpretations that formed us are exposed, and our true selves—a unifying process lured forward by beauty—emerge. Again, the implications are both personal and social as the very principalities and powers of this world are reconciled to the mind of Christ. This process of transformation is nothing less than the emergence of a whole new creation in which all things are of God (2 Corinthians 5:18). Mimetic atonement becomes the encounter in which every desire I have allowed to form me dissolves, and consequently, I am undone and made anew. It is the event in which I am re-formed as I come face to face with my origin, the authentic desire that imagined me and brought me forth—in the God who is love.

6

Processing Consciousness

Let's return to the larger implications of all this and look at some further details about consciousness. Whiteheadian process philosophy and mimetic theory overlap in their interest in human consciousness. Both explore the emergence of consciousness, the significance of desire, symbolic thought processes, and self-awareness. The intensification and complexification of processes produce novelty for both Girard and Whitehead. In *Things Hidden Since the Foundation of the World*, Girard speaks of the "intensification of mimesis" and how "new and more complex forms" of societies become birthed through the "intensification of mimetic rivalry" that leads to the scapegoating mechanism.[1] For Whitehead, as we have seen, every process has two categories of relations: the determinate *physical* prehensions and the *conceptual* prehensions that allows the actuality to break free from inherited determinacies and introduce novel possibilities. Higher intellectual capacities, such as human consciousness, will have a greater capacity for complexity, the direct result of entertaining a wider variety of possibilities. Moreover, the process of

---

1. Girard, *Things Hidden since the Foundation of the World,* 96, 97, 94.

115

harmonization of a more complex variety of contrasts will inevitable be more intense.

Thus, we can see that human consciousness is characterized by the creative capacity to break free from inherited forms and realize novel possibilities, resulting in more complex and intense experiences. Judith Jones, who interprets Whitehead's work through the lens of *Intensity*, notes: "There is a greater degree of freedom on the part of the entities involved to entertain the relevance of possibilities somewhat remote to merely physical experience."[2] We'll now explore the development of human consciousness from the perspective of the intensification and complexification of desire, symbolism, and self-awareness.

Intensification of Desire

Whitehead describes consciousness as "a mode of attention," which "provides the extreme of selective emphasis."[3] The phrase *selective emphasis* implies preference which is the function of appetition/desire. He, therefore, sees a close connection between art and consciousness, because we can see art as a process of selective harmonization. In this creative process, we filter all available elements and assign them values so that the vagueness of some emphasize and clarify others, resulting in a unique perspective. This aesthetic movement begins in the dim and "unconscious activities of experience" but finds an outlet in the specialization of consciousness.[4] Whitehead concludes: "Consciousness itself is the product of art in its lowliest form. For it results from the influx of ideality into its contrast with reality, with the purpose of reshaping the latter into a finite, select appearance."[5] Preference or desire permeates the entire process.

---

2. Judith A. Jones, *Intensity: An Essay in Whiteheadian Ontology*. (Nashville, TN: Vanderbilt University Press, 1998), 134.

3. Whitehead, *Adventures of Ideas*, 270.

4. Ibid.

5. Ibid., 271.

David Ray Griffin, a Whiteheadian scholar, identifies phases of mentality that lead to the complexity of human consciousness. Whitehead's concept of *appetition* plays a particularly relevant role here in our inquiry. Griffin states: "Mentality is essentially *appetition*, either for or against some possible form of experience. It can be a blind urge to realize, or avoid, some form of feeling."[6] Appetition is a mode of attention, for attention results from finding some elements more attractive than others. Modes of attention—the intensity and complexity of desire—differentiate between different levels of consciousness. As I elaborated in the previous chapter, we find an intensification and complexification of appetition in higher-order organisms.

Girard postulates a concrete event in which passions intensified to the point of an ecstatic release, resulting in the slaughter of the scapegoat. Let's consider how this might look, harmonized with Whitehead's insights. When the trance-like violence subsides and the participants see the body of their victim, a catalytic moment unfolds, an opportunity for them to contemplate the consequences of unrestrained passion. We can see how this moment could have created an ideal situation for a higher order of consciousness to emerge. It's worth reminding ourselves of Whitehead's perspective on the intensification of desire: "The higher forms of intellectual experience only arise when there are complex integrations, and re-integrations, of mental and physical experience. Reason then appears as a criticism of appetitions. It is a second-order type of mentality. It is the appetitions of appetitions."[7] Both Girard and Whitehead recognize a connection between the emergence of human consciousness and the intensification of desire.

---

6. David Ray Griffin, *Unsnarling the World-Knot: Consciousness, Freedom, and the Mind-Body Problem.* (Eugene, OR: Wipf and Stock Publishers, 2007), 129.

7. Whitehead, *The Function of Reason*, Location 361.

Intensification of Symbolism

For Whitehead, every process has an interiority in which physical causes and conceptual possibilities become reconciled into a novel unity. For physical feelings to be harmonized with possibilities, some measure of abstraction and symbolization proves necessary. This process whereby the two modes fuse into one perception is what Whitehead calls symbolic reference.[8] Consequently, for him, every process is symbolic. Roland Faber describes the symbolic reference as holding "the treasures and wonders of the passage of meaning and the meaning of the passionate passage of feelings; and of symbolic revolution—that it generates the revolutionary indeterminacy that allows for the appearance for novelty and its integration into the process."[9] Significantly, Whitehead thought that "an occasional revolution in symbolism is required," and this leap is exactly what Girard hypothesized happened in the scapegoating process.[10]

Symbolic reference enables freedom, novelty, and error. In fact, the very capacity for error marks higher forms of intelligence: "human perception is subject to error, because, in respect to those components most clearly in consciousness, it is interpretative."[11] Thus the very mechanism that enables novelty and freedom also inevitably enables error. Whitehead recognizes more complex forms of consciousness as *living* occasions: "A LIVING occasion is characterized by a flash of novelty among the appetitions of its mental pole."[12] These novel appetitions (novel instances of desire) are com-

---

8. Alfred North Whitehead, *Symbolism, Its Meaning and Effect: Barbour-Page Lectures, University of Virginia, 1927.* (New York: Fordham University Press, 1985), 18.

9. Roland Faber, *The Mind of Whitehead: Adventure in Ideas*, (Eugene, OR: Pickwick Publications, an imprint of Wipf and Stock Publishers. Kindle Edition,) 85.

10. Whitehead, Symbolism, 61.

11. Whitehead, *Process and Reality*, 168.

12. Ibid., 184.

plex conceptual prehensions. The intensification of desire and the complexification of the symbolic process show two perspectives on the same process. For we can see that desire is the *conceptual* prehension of possibilities, and symbolic reference is the way in which these possibilities are reconciled with *physical* prehensions. The more possibilities are considered, the more complex the process of symbolism, harmonization, and interpretation becomes. So, higher orders of consciousness exhibit greater freedom, novelty, and interpretive error.

For Girard, the process of scapegoating provides the catalyst that sparks a revolution in symbolic thought. In this moment the primitive community breaks free from the natural order, and thereby, all inherited symbolic references are freed from pre-defined meaning. He calls this a crisis of undifferentiation.[13] Subsequently, the corpse of the surrogate victim becomes a focal point in which all the symbols are reassembled. The abundance of contrasts—chaos and order, death and life, violence and peace—all become contained and embodied in the victim. Girard proposes a concrete event in which Whitehead's more abstract speculations could be verified. Indeed, we have all the same elements present: intensified desire, an abundance of contrasts, and a revolution of symbolic reference. The consequences are surprising. A new social order becomes possible because the community has invented a mechanism for controlling violence. Girard shows how ritual reinforces the new symbolic order, eventually finding a new form of expression in language and myth.

However, in this scenario all the novelty comes about because of errors in interpretation. In Girard's narrative, the community misdiagnoses the problem of increased frustration and violence. Not

---

13. Girard, *Evolution and Conversion*, 42.

able to recognize the nature of their desire, the crowd incorrectly identifies the scapegoat as the reason for their frustration. Moreover, the interpretative errors continue and intensify as ritual and myth add layers of meaning to the events. The victim becomes both demonized as the cause of the chaos and divinized as the cause of the subsequent peace. The novel gods, religions, cultures, and civilizations birthed through this creative process remain vulnerable to the interpretive errors that birthed them.

Whitehead seems also to intuitively seek just such a catalytic event that precedes the revolution in symbolic thought. He thinks that the practice of agriculture played a significant role, but he's not totally satisfied with such an explanation. He seems to grasp for a more concrete event to explain the emergence of mental attention: "There must have been some instances to provoke attention." And again, he says: "I am seeking to determine the dividing line after which the curiously quick acceleration of civilized thought may conceivably have arisen."[14] For Girard, the body of the victim, produced by scapegoating violence, provides the community with exactly the kind of object or event that "provoked attention" and became the dividing line after which symbolic thought could develop. I think Girard's solution in positing the crisis of undifferentiation and a primordial scapegoating scenario may satisfy many of Whitehead's adventurous questions and intuitions.

The symbolic revolution, however it happened, enabled a broader perspective and clearer distinction between past, present, and future in human consciousness, thereby increasing the range of meaning-making possibilities and the complexity of desire. Complex consciousness reconsiders past decisions and envision future ideals.

---

14. Whitehead, *Adventures of ideas*, 110.

Appetition underwent a transformation into the kind of desire that extends beyond immediate satisfaction and reaches for grander, distant goals. In this more complex exemplification of appetition, desire persists beyond the boundaries of a single occasion. Whitehead terms this extension of desire, *vision*.[15] Vision here means the ability to see beyond the immediate reality and envision the ideal. The ideal differs from the present precisely because it's more desirable. Vision of the ideal represents a complex form of desire. We can recognize the intimate link between desire and identity in that both are patterns of similarity that persists from occasion to occasion.

We can easily see the evolutionary advantage of both hindsight and foresight, for these would allow for better preparation to exploit opportunities. Whitehead observes: "The conceptual entertainment of unrealized possibility becomes a major factor in human mentality."[16] We are able to regret missed opportunities and, consequently, prepare better for similar future opportunities. The experience of regret serves as an example of a new complexity of awareness in which we reconsider how negative prehensions have influenced our development. William James expressed it succinctly: "in every hinderance of desire the sense of an ideal presence which is absent in fact…is even more notoriously there."[17]

A natural outflow of this increased meaning-making capacity within a social environment would be a new form of expression—language. The symbolization and interpretation that happens in conceptual prehension/feeling finds a new complexity in language. In Whitehead's metaphysical framework, language need not be limited

---

15. 'appetition,' which in its higher exemplifications we term 'vision.' (Whitehead, *Process and Reality*, 212.)

16. Whitehead, *Modes of Thought*, 26.

17. William James. *A Pluralistic Universe*. (Halls of Wisdom, Kindle Edition), Loc 2030.

to logical description of our world but it also intensifies experience. He states: "It is more important that a proposition be interesting than that it be true. This statement is almost a tautology. For the energy of operation of a proposition in an occasion of experience is its interest, and its importance."[18]

Decrying how language becomes impoverished if only used for the communication of logic, he writes: "The interest in logic, dominating overintellectualized philosophers, has obscured the main function of propositions in the nature of things. They are not primarily for belief, but for feeling at the physical level of unconsciousness."[19] Within Whitehead's scheme, the category of *propositions* forms part of the fabric of reality. For him, language (as part of this category) not only connects us with reality but is part of the creative advance of our world. Stephen T. Franklin, in considering the connection between Whitehead and the theory of language, writes:

> Language is a form of symbolism. An actual entity uses symbolism whenever it uses one element in its world to elicit, promote, foster, enhance, identify, or isolate another factor in its experience....In particular, language is a form of symbolism...that promotes the grasping (that is, the inclusion or prehension) of propositions...Thus language, as it symbolizes our feelings of propositions, not only adds to our freedom and increases our capacity to shape our own world, but it also links us to the concrete physical world out of which we emerge.[20]

---

18. Whitehead, *Adventures of Ideas,* 244.

19. Whitehead, *Process and Reality,* 186.

20. Michel Weber and Will Desmond, eds. *Handbook of Whiteheadian Process Thought, Volume 2,* (Frankfurt / Lancaster: ontos verlag, Process Thought X1 & X2, 2008), 12.

The narrative capacity inherent in all of nature finds new intensity, new width, new depth, new complexity, and a new form of expression in human consciousness.

Intensification of Self-Awareness

A third unique aspect of human consciousness is self-awareness. The event of becoming a self in non-human entities can be likened to a mirror: The entity receives (prehends) the influence of other entities, interprets those influences in relation to possibilities, and uniquely reflects them in its own becoming. Whitehead notes: "An entity is actual, when it has significance for itself."[21] In human consciousness, however, the mirror turns in on itself, opening a whole new dimension of complexity. "The private psychological field," says Whitehead, "is merely the event considered from its own standpoint."[22] The meaning-making process, which is operative in all occasions, becomes aware of itself in human consciousness. Adding this layer of self-reflective complexity creates a much richer meaning-making matrix. It allows for an internal conversation and an increased capacity for rational meaning. Thus, our narrative capacity gains internal depth. Some psychologists refer to the conscious and unconscious as two systems or two languages. Based on this view, every experience will be inscribed twice, allowing it to be interpreted in two fundamentally different ways.[23] Conscious self-awareness not only gives us new insight into ourselves but also into others who

---

21. Whitehead, *Process and Reality*, 25.

22. Whitehead, *Science and the Modern World*, 150.

23. "There may be a totally different inscription of the same signifier in consciousness and in the unconscious. These inscriptions are the same on the plane of the signifier, but they are, on the other hand, different in that they turn their battery to occupy topographically different places. That a certain signifying formation can be at one level or another is precisely what will ensure it a different import in the chain as a whole." Anika Lemaire, *Jacques Lacan*. Trans. David Macy (Abington, UK: Routledge, 1991).

are like us. A new awareness of self and the interiority of others *like* myself opens new possibilities of meaning and intensifies narrative capacity, including ethical meaning.

Max Velmans, a psychologist, ventures the idea that "consciousness may be a naturally occurring feature of all neural representations."[24] Synapses have the important function of filtering and inhibiting the vast amounts of information streaming into the brain. The more complex the brain, the more necessary it would be to filter consciousness to include only the most necessary information. "In this case, rather than adding something to unconscious representations to make them conscious, attention would correspond to a highly selective release of consciousness from inhibition."[25] What we experience as conscious awareness, therefore, is not a new type of process, but a reconfiguration of the unconscious type of experience Whitehead identifies as a feeling, a prehension.

To Velmans' helpful perspective I would add that conscious attention also processes information/feelings differently. Conscious awareness fulfills a different function than general information processing. Interestingly, Whitehead thinks the unconscious has a closer connection to reality than the conscious because the conscious relies more on interpretation. And more interpretation also increases the likelihood of misinterpretation. In Whitehead's terminology, *Appearance* refers to an interpretation of reality.

It [the conscious] raises the importance of the final Appearance relative to that of the initial Reality....What leaps into conscious attention is a mass of presuppositions about

---

24. Weber, *Process Approaches to Consciousness in Psychology, Neuroscience, and Philosophy of Mind.* Kindle Location 501.

25. Ibid., Kindle Location 503.

Reality rather than the intuitions of Reality itself. It is here that the liability to error arises. The deliverances of clear and distinct consciousness require criticism by reference to elements in experience which are neither clear nor distinct. On the contrary, they are dim, massive, and important.[26]

Girard, too, recognizes that the truth often makes itself known unconsciously. In analyzing what he calls "texts of persecution," he notes that: "For the social historian reliable testimony…will never be as valuable as the unreliable testimony of persecutors, or their accomplices, which reveals more because of its unconscious nature."[27] The more conscious we are about constructing a narrative, the more interpretative the process becomes, enabling both novelty and error. We have already established that levels of consciousness differentiate by the complexity of desire. Moreover, we have different levels of interpretation between the conscious and unconscious, with desire formative in every act of interpretation.

The process view of reality doesn't diminish the uniqueness of human personhood but gives it new meaning. Instead of an indefinable spirit or mind-like substance, the human self is a unifying process that preserves and expands identity. In contrasting the substance view of personhood with the process view, Rescher writes:

The unity of self comes to be seen as a unity of process—of one large megaprocess that encompasses many smaller ones in its makeup. We arrive at a view of mind that dispenses with the Cartesian "ghost in the machine" and looks to

---

26. Whitehead, *Adventures of Ideas*, 270.

27. René Girard, *The Scapegoat*. Translated by Yvonne Freccero. (Baltimore: The Johns Hopkins University Press, Kindle Edition), 8.

the unity of mind as a unity of functioning—of operations rather than operators.[28]

Note that desire guides both the broadening of narrative capacity explored in the previous point and the deepening of this meaning-making process. Desire gives direction and form to interpretation and as such proves essential for the unity of process and the unity of self.

---

28. Rescher, *Process Metaphysics: An Introduction to Process Philosophy*, 109.

7

Ritual, Religion, and Civilization

In a section of his book *Adventures of Ideas*, Whitehead speculates about the origins of civilization.[1] His intuitions have remarkable points of convergence with Girard's ideas. Whitehead similarly rejects the idea that civilization began with a social contract.[2] Rather, he perceives that communities were dominated by "modes of behaviour" and "inrushes of emotion." Rational thoughts and ideas developed mainly as "justification...of a pre-existing situation." In *Religion in the Making*, he again emphasizes the priority of emotion and ritual in the origin of religion: "when we go far enough back, belief and rationalization are completely negligible...Belief then makes its appearance as explanatory of the complex of ritual and emotion, and in this appearance of belief we may discern the germ of rationalization."[3] These intuitions about the origins of religion fall into agreement with Girard's understanding. Both Whitehead and Girard recognize ritual as the origin of religion.

However, their explanation for the origin of ritual differs. Whitehead describes ritual as an activity operative in both human

---

1. Whitehead, *Adventures of ideas*, 241.

2. Ibid., 110.

3. Whitehead. *Religion in the Making*. 9.

and animal communities.[4] Consequently, he focuses on the mimetic repetition and enjoyment of the activity and doesn't recognize the role of scapegoating violence in the formation of human rituals. (His explanation, however, does not exclude this possibility.) As we have previously noted, Whitehead considers ritual a form of art in which a person or community can relive the intensity of an experience without the immediacy of danger.

Girard sees ritual as a reenactment of the events that culminated in scapegoating violence or sacrifice. Both the threatening chaos and the magical solution—the sacrifice that stopped the uncontrolled violence and brought peace—form part of many rituals. Girard gives attention to the actual events that lead to the practice of ritual, while Whitehead recognizes the more general principle behind the practice. But in the end, they agree that ritual "emerges as a way for humans to relive in tranquility what was initially experienced as a struggle for survival."[5] For Whitehead, the struggle for survival could refer to a simple activity such as the hunt for food. For Girard, the struggle for survival would refer to the uncontrolled violence that threatened to consume the whole community.

Girard and Whitehead have other areas of overlap in complementary insights. Despite his emphasis upon creativity, scapegoating, too, appears as a theme in Whitehead's thought. Images of solitariness constitute the heart of religious importance for him: "Prometheus chained to his rock, Mahomet brooding in the desert, the meditations of Buddha, the solitary Man on the Cross. It belongs to the depth of the religious spirit to have felt forsaken, even by God."[6] Although Whitehead might not have consciously thought

---

4. Ibid., 20.

5. Weber, *Handbook of Whiteheadian Process Thought Volume 1*, 44.

6. Whitehead, *Religion in the Making*, 19.

of, or named, scapegoating violence as the origin of religion and ritual, the images he perceives to be the heart of religion—solitariness
and feeling forsaken—are unconsciously saturated in scapegoating
symbolism. Girard, more explicitly, shows how the collective act of
scapegoating murder would be a spontaneous act driven by passion
rather than reason. Yet, the peace that follows creates a solitary space
in which passion recedes and reflection begins. The ideas and myths
that are born in this space are indeed occupied with the justification of "a pre-existing situation"—the fact of scapegoating violence.
Here we see striking correlations with Whitehead's more general
intuitions.

In summary, although Whitehead didn't recognize the significance of scapegoating violence in the formation of ritual, religion,
culture, and civilizations, many of his intuitions were, nonethe-
less, consistent with Girard's theory that developed decades later.
As demonstrated in Chapter 5, Whitehead recognized and searched
for a catalytic event after which rational thought developed, but he
never found it. Girard provides a theory of exactly such an event.

8

Theological and Narrative Harmonies

Joining Whitehead's cosmological thought with Girard's anthropological insights creates a larger narrative. The first goal in creating a vibrant harmony, according to Whitehead, would be to avoid any "painful clash," meaning each narrative should be able to remain true to itself. That would accomplish what Whitehead calls "the minor form of beauty." The second goal aims at utilizing the new contrasts created between these narratives to create new harmonies. That would achieve the "intensity" that Whitehead requires for the "major form" of a beautiful harmony.

I have attempted to bring Whitehead's and Girard's narratives together, to create new insight and possibilities of meaning. The essence of Girard's theological contribution can be summarized as providing an anthropologically-based view of the message of Scripture, culminating in the events of Jesus' life, death, and resurrection. But let's first understand the relationship between anthropology and theology. Anthropology is the science that considers all the dimensions of being human, including the processes that made us human (hominization), the origins of religion (religious studies and the philosophy of religion), and the way we live (sociology.) Studying these areas requires no commitment to any particular religion. Theology, in contrast, assumes some form of faith commitment as it is rooted in the conviction of God's self-revelation.

Girard did not consider himself a theologian but an anthropologist. He developed a thoroughly anthropological account of human experience, including our experience of the sacred. He even explains the origins of religion and culture from this anthropological perspective. In this context all the gods are idols, human inventions born from the intense experiences of scapegoating violence. Scapegoating violence becomes transformed into sacred violence, or sacrifice, as religions develop to contain violence. When Girard started reading the Bible, he did so from this anthropological perspective he had used in reading myths and other texts. However, instead of dismissing the Bible as simply another iteration of the ancient origin myths, he came to recognize that it gradually and persistently exposed the message of these myths.

Girard shows that although the biblical stories have similar structures to many origin myths, they pause and focus on the areas that the myths are blind to, questioning the pervading wisdom of the time. The scriptures *reinterpret* the events of violent scapegoating, enabling us to see their meaning in retrospect. In the story of Jesus, we find the most complete and surprising revelation of what has been hidden "since the foundation of the world." The result is a profound subversion of meaning by the biblical texts. This revelation, Girard believes, can only be explained as the result of a superior intelligence, of one who stood outside the scapegoating cycle—Jesus. Girard explains:

[T]he Gospels cannot be the product of a work purely elaborated within the effervescent milieu of the early Christians. At the text's origins there must have been someone outside

132

the group, a higher intelligence which is master of the disciples and inspired their writings. As we succeed in reconstituting mimetic theory in… the words attributed to Jesus, we are disclosing the traces of that intelligence, not the reflections of the disciples.[1]

We could say that precisely because Jesus was fully human, he could bring the anthropological story to a crescendo. I see how an incarnational theology gains an anthropological width from this perspective. Human idols are undone by Jesus's revelation, and it simultaneously brings into view the God that is not the product of our invention. Therefore, Girard offers a radical critique of religion and sacrifice with significant theological implications. Notice how Girard sheds new light on the two fundamental issues with which the scriptures wrestle: first, we have the attempt to articulate the nature of the human problem. What causes dysfunctional relationship with God, creation, and one another? Second, the scriptures explore ways in which the problem could be resolved.

Girard's insight into the nature of human desire allows him to uniquely diagnose the problem of conflict and violence. Anthropologically, the problem posed is even more profound than that of religion or culture. Humans were violent before they were religious. The very processes that formed us have left a mark, a bias, or an inability to see our part in the problem. Indeed, Girard sees his theory as a sort of scientific version of the traditional doctrine of original sin. But the idea of original sin takes on new possibilities of meaning from his anthropological perspective. In his narrative scenario, humans did not begin in a perfect utopian paradise and

---

1. René Girard, *The Scapegoat,* trans. Yvonne Freccero (Baltimore: The Johns Hopkins University Press, 1986), 162.

subsequently fell. Rather, in the process of our evolution, a fundamental misinterpretation became embodied in our existence and gave violence an undeserved justification.

This misinterpretation formed part of the evolution of religion and civilization. Consequently, Girard's critique of the nature of desire extends to a critique of the formation of religion and civilization itself. Religion and civilization institutionalized this flaw in the human meaning-making process. Furthermore, many concepts we hold to be sacred within religion, such as sacrifice, originate in a profound misunderstanding of scapegoating violence. As such, Jesus, through his life and death and resurrection, didn't affirm the religious sentiments of his world but brought them to an end through a radical reinterpretation of their meaning. Consequently, the practice of animal sacrifice ceased after Christ exposed and redefined the concept within the new Christian community that embraced his teachings. We can see how Girard's ideas have wide theological implications, including the way in which we understand the idea of atonement.

Girard diagnoses the fundamental human problem as misrecognition and misinterpretation of the nature of desire, leading to violence and resulting in religion and civilization built on this flawed and vulnerable foundation. But how we interpret our world isn't something accidental to our nature. Our interpretations, right or wrong, shape us. The solution to misinterpretation involves a reinterpretation of—and therefore a transformation of—desire. For Girard, the revolutionary new interpretation revealed by Christ becomes the foundation for a new way of being human.

We can see that nothing in this mimetic narrative fundamentally contradicts process philosophy. Girard's narrative can retain its freedom as an element in a larger story—we have no "painful clash." Next, let us look at Whitehead's theological contribution. Its essence can be summarized as providing us a view of reality that transforms our perspective of God in addition to human beings. Whitehead's theological claims are more explicit than Girard's, yet he frames what he has to say about God with great humility in the final chapter of *Process and Reality*. He reminds us that these ideas he offers about God are only a perspective produced by an incomplete framework of understanding:

> [W]e must investigate dispassionately what the metaphysical principles, here developed, require on these points, as to the nature of God. There is nothing here in the nature of proof. There is merely the confrontation of the theoretic system with a certain rendering of the facts. But the unsystematized report upon the facts is itself highly controversial, and the system is confessedly inadequate. The deductions from it in this particular sphere of thought cannot be looked upon as more than suggestions as to how the problem is transformed in the light of that system.[2]

Despite his humble framing, Whitehead's "suggestions" unveil a profound and bold vision of God that has subsequently inspired many theologians to further expound it. Perceiving God as *process* rather than substance changes how we understand God's relationship with the world. A large part of Western theology embraces a substantialist philosophical approach, but it has come with inherent inconsistencies in which God-as-substance becomes the exception

---

2. Whitehead, *Process and Reality*, 343.

to every definition of substance.[3] This poses a logical and metaphysical problem.

In contrast, Whitehead states that within the process approach, "God is not to be treated as an exception to all metaphysical principles, invoked to save their collapse. He is their chief exemplification."[4] Thus, understanding God's involvement in the world becomes simplified and consistent with our understanding of reality. Instead of a separate substance intervening in world events, God can be understood as a unifying process and intimately involved in every event. As such, God can be seen as deeply involved in the beauty, the intelligibility, and the progress we discern in our world.

Whitehead's speculations have profound implications. When our fundamental perceptions of the nature of reality change, every concept of God changes with it. A new vision emerges of God's power, knowledge, and creativity. What we mean by God as person, God as redeemer, God as incarnate, God's transcendence, and God's immanence—all these become transformed from this new perspective.

Consequently, process theology brings something new to traditional theological conceptions or, at least, highlights some nuanced aspects that were well hidden. Traditional theology often favors some qualities and excludes others from the character of God. For instance, God has been perceived as eternal and not temporal, changeless rather than affected by the events in our world. Process theology, in contrast, perceives God as one in whom these contrasts find harmony. We find qualities in God that are indeed eternally changeless, yet God is also deeply affected by relationship and the

---

3. See Rescher, Nicholas. *Process Metaphysics: An Introduction to Process Philosophy*, 154.

4. Whitehead, *Process and Reality*, 343.

events of our world. Keith Ward, a contemporary philosopher and theologian, recognizing the uniqueness of Whitehead, writes: "For the first time in the history of philosophy, a major theistic philosopher not only stresses the reality of the finite, material world unequivocally, but also makes temporality a thing of positive value, a condition of real creativity."[5]

For Whitehead, God is both transcendent and immanent, present in every occasion, yet luring the world beyond its current reality into transcendent beauty. As we concluded earlier, we find creativity as a relational activity within this process view. As such, God will be involved in every creative movement and, simultaneously, God is actually being created *by* these relational movements. This changes our concept of God's power. God's power is never absolute—separate from creatures and God's loving nature. instead, it is co-creative, shared with all creation.

Nothing in this Whiteheadian process narrative finds itself fundamentally contradictory to Girardian mimetic theory. Once again, we have a narrative which can retain its freedom as an element in an enlarged story—we have no "painful clash" from this end either. Now having two narratives, each with its own integrity, we can move on to the second goal of creating a vibrant harmony between these discourses—namely, creating new contrasts and possibilities for what Whitehead calls novel harmonies. We'll begin by considering whether their narrative trajectories can be complimentary.

Narrative Trajectory

Whitehead's cosmology provides a rich and fruitful source for creation theology, for its most fundamental characteristic is a creative

---

5. Keith Ward, *Rational Theology and the Creativity of God* (Oxford: Basil Blackwell, 1985), 227.

advance toward beauty. For Whitehead, the trajectory of the cosmic narrative is lured toward novel harmonies. For Girard, scapegoating violence serves as a generative event behind the evolution of humanity, including religion and culture. However, we would be mistaken if we consider the scapegoating event as the only event that influences the direction of the Girardian narrative. The mimetic story would be incomplete without emphasizing the creative mimetic capacities that are prior to scapegoating, and the radical subversion of the misinterpretations of violence and the new symbolic revolution that culminates in the death and resurrection of Christ. Girard doesn't really talk about the first, but does talk about the second. But we can see that the story doesn't begin with scapegoating violence but with mimetic desire, which opens us to more intimate relationships with others and God. And the story doesn't end with violence but with a subversive new way of interpreting human relationships, what he calls "the Kingdom of God." Although Girard's theory does not explicitly propose a creation theology or develop this alternative to violence very much, we do find it undeniably present in the trajectory of his narrative.

Remember, for Whitehead, the interpretive nature of every process means that novelty and error, freedom and danger, go hand in hand. At times it is the very error in interpretation that leads to something creatively new. For a concrete example, look at the misinterpretations surrounding the scapegoating event, for they result in the novelties of ritual, religion, and civilization. Girard provides another concrete example of how God lures the story forward when he demonstrates how the biblical narrative exposes our flawed misinterpretations and offers a new way of making meaning.

John Haught, a theologian who incorporates many process perspectives into his work, also sees a narrative progression in our cosmic story.[6] He notes how many of the attempts made by authors of "Big History," a genre that connects the relatively short human story with the larger cosmic story, have failed to recognize "*how one stage interpenetrates the others.*"[7] Subjectivity opens up an inner story that is often completely ignored by those who only recognize a naturalistic explanation:

> Big History scholars locate—and deflate—the human story by placing it against the backdrop of the universe's spatial and temporal immensity. This is a useful point of view, but not the only one. The universe, after all, includes subjects, hidden centers of experience whose significance cannot be measured by science or captured by purely historical reporting.[8]

Haught believes that a narrative that coherently connects the big history of our cosmos with the emergence of human consciousness and religion can only be achieved when we recognize that "*subjectivity was already implicit in the physical properties of the early universe.*"[9]

Anthony Bartlett, a Girardian theologian, recognizes the significance of this need for a narrative trajectory: he argues that the greatest value of Girard's theory and indeed of the Bible, lies in how it provides a whole new way of constructing meaning.[10] Many of the process perspectives we have explored so far also find resonance in Bartlett's view. He sees *relation,* and the possibilities of meaning

---

6. Haught, *The New Cosmic Story: Inside Our Awakening Universe.*

7. Ibid., 1.

8. Ibid., 2.

9. Ibid., 16.

10. Bartlett, *Theology Beyond Metaphysics.*

it opens, as more constitutive of reality than *things*. Moreover, for Bartlett, meaning derives not from a pre-existent metaphysical world, but is created from within the relationship of the present reality.[11] As such, he shows how the Bible's most extraordinary effect would be the gradual re-creation of human language and meaning itself. Girard has shown the violent origins of language. But for Bartlett, the Bible begins a process of revealing a wholly new possibility of meaning-making:

> Love is the revelatory engine bringing us the truth of the human condition, but that is exactly the point. It is divine and human love which shows us at one and the same time the dysfunction and the transformation of the anthropos, giving us together human reality misspoken, and human reality re-spoken and remade.[12]

For Bartlett, then, the Bible essentially aims not to give us a set of true ideas, but to expose the violent origin of our meaning-making capacities and at the same time offer us a new basis for creating meaning.[13] This radical transformation of the very structure of meaning then points to the nature of God.

---

11. "Relation (or the most specific version of this we will arrive at—hypostasis) is the term which allows the sign to reach out beyond present being to completely new possibilities. But it does so from within present existence because it is a real relationship, made possible by Christ. To understand this involves a shift from "things" and "ideas" as fundamental, to seeing signs and relations as truly constitutive." Ibid.,18.

12. Ibid., 45.

13. "The argument then is definitely not that the Bible somehow achieves a transparent intellectual idea, or a set of ideas, but rather that it intervenes in the root structure of signs and meaning itself, diverting the river of human semiosis from its original spring or, in fact, providing a new one. This is a much more challenging claim. The Bible builds on the fluidity of human meaning, arriving finally at a form that is genuinely radical and new." ibid., 51.

In Girard's thought, scapegoating violence served as the first pattern of formative events that shaped the environment in which we could create meaning. It shaped our understanding, our language, and our experience of ourselves, others, and God. Inherent in the very origin of this framework we find blind-spots, misunderstandings, and a limitation to the meanings we could create. The justification of violence forms part of the fabric of this framework of misinterpretation.

Christ's exposure of these "principalities and powers"[14] opens the possibility of a new language. From this Girardian perspective, Christ transforms the very structures by which we create meaning. He does this by taking us back to the original event that demanded our attention and so formed human consciousness—the body of the victim. But in Jesus, this crucified victim, rather than seeking revenge, forgives.[15] The resurrection proves the innocence of the victim and the guilt of the perpetrators, yet beyond this, the invitation to receive forgiveness becomes an invitation to transcend the cycles of violence and the old framework of meaning-making. We are offered a new, more expansive, and more honest framework of language. In this framework we find no forceful control; rather, it is love's vision of beauty that has a persuasive influence on the trajectory of our narratives. This resonates with Whitehead's thought that history has a trajectory that reduces violence and favors persuasive power:

The history of ideas is a history of mistakes. But through all mistakes it is also the history of the gradual purification of

---

14. See Ephesians 3:10 and 1 Corinthians 2:8.
15. See Acts 2:29-39.

conduct. When there is progress in the development of favourable order, we find conduct protected from relapse into brutalization by the increasing agency of ideas consciously entertained. In this way Plato is justified in his saying. The creation of the world—that is to say, the world of civilized order—is the victory of persuasion over force.[16]

Girard's concept of conversion represents a radical new development in human meaning-making by exposing the violent origins of language and introducing a whole new way of creating meaning oriented toward greater beauty. Here we have the good news section of mimetic theory that has not always received the emphasis from Girardians it deserves. Girard himself remained true to his stated focus on the negative in his last book, *Battling to the End*. The impression that Girard is rather pessimistic seems justified with statements such as this:

> one could argue that the verse "when the Son of Man comes, will he find faith on earth?" is still too full of hope. The Revelation has failed: in a certain manner it has not been heard.[17]

Yet in the last chapter, he again acknowledges that the revelation of Christ changed human history: "It is thus that God revealed himself in his Son, that religion was confirmed once and for all, thereby changing the course of human history."[18] However, it is difficult to

---

16. Whitehead, *Adventures of Ideas*, 25.
17. Girard, *Battling to the End*, 47.
18. Ibid., 217.

see what the good news is for Girard, seeing that he says the revelation of Christ removed the limitation of violence (the sacrificial
system) and thereby makes the escalation to extremes and an apoc-
alyptic end more likely. Girard remains enigmatic and ambiguous
on these points, especially in articulating how the life, death and
resurrection of Jesus actually ushers in an alternative to violence.

Bartlett is one example of a Girardian scholar developing the
positive theological implications of mimetic theory and I hope to
add to this emphasis, having demonstrated that mimetic cycles form
part of a creative advance. I'm not claiming that positive mimesis is
more valid than negative mimesis or that the good news of transformed meaning is more valid than the sobering history of human
violence. Both good and evil are actual and possible—but I am saying that the overall trajectory is towards beauty. The significance of
Christ's victory over evil and the unveiling of a whole new creation
must be emphasized even amid the cycles of violence, for that is the
revelation that can transform our world. We are reminded of the
counterintuitive strategy of God, to save those who hear through the
"foolishness of declaring the good news" (1 Cor. 1:21).

The creation theology implicitly present in Girard's narrative can
be made more explicit if we apply Whiteheadian cosmology to it, for
it helps us understand the relationship between interpretation, error,
and the creation of novelty present in every process. This creative
emphasis also clarifies the fact that no one event can be interpreted
correctly without considering the larger context. The scapegoating
mechanism should therefore find its meaning in the narrative as a
whole. Consequently, I am saying that the subversion of meaning
brought about by the biblical scriptures and the revelation of Christ
places the scapegoating event in its proper context. In this context,
mimetic theory represents not an ontology of violence but a story

of creative love in which God enters the human drama to suffer and undo our misinterpretations.

Process philosophy also clarifies the immanence, vulnerability, and involvement of God in the development of the human narrative—God has always been present in every moment, opening new possibilities of meaning even as we have misunderstood events and given violence undue justification. God shares in the world's experience—both the joy and the suffering. Yet, God's presence is not overbearing but participatory, even in a history that contains the scapegoat mechanism. This kind of God opens the opportunity for humans to co-create their reality and affirms that our choices truly matter. Such a God draws the story forward, not by external force, but by the persistent influence of the divine vision of beauty and goodness.

The Significance of Jesus

Whitehead recognized a profound beauty in the message of Jesus. In his exploration of beauty, he provides for degrees of beauty, understanding there to be lower levels of beauty not necessarily having a relation to truth. But he notes, "When Appearance has to Reality, in some important direct sense, a truth-relation, there is a security about the Beauty attained, that is to say, a pledge for the future."[19] The event of scapegoating, from a Whiteheadian perspective, would lack a higher degree of beauty because it is dependent on a misinterpretation of events. It, therefore, has no "security" or "pledge for the future." For Whitehead, higher degrees of beauty must have a relationship with truth. For Girard, this higher degree of beauty occurs in the event of Christ, for Christ exposes the scapegoating process.

---

19. Whitehead, *Adventures of ideas*, 267.

Similarly, Whitehead sees the significance of Jesus in his victory over violence:

> It is sufficient to note that the Gospels exhibit an astounding beauty of moral feeling, and of delicate sensibility. It is the tale of the victory of love over brutality and hatred. It stretches from the Babe in a Manger, to the Man wandering homeless, to the Man on the Cross. It expresses his victory over brute force....It was a revelation of the religious ideal, respecting the action and re-action between cosmological thought, and emotion, and purposeful activity. It discarded brutality, and was untouched by hatred.[20]

In the above quote, Whitehead refers to the event of Christ as a revelation, something which correlates with Girard's view. And the content of the revelation, for both thinkers, has to do with the victory of love over violence. Although Jesus is not essential to Whitehead's metaphysics, when he applies metaphysics to actual human history, he sees a movement from force to persuasion that finds a crescendo—a "revelation of the religious ideal"—in the story of Jesus Christ. The power and glory of Christ's life "lies in its absence of force."[21]

In another instance, Whitehead explores the progression of religion from a communal practice whose purpose is simply to avoid harm, into the concept of an individual transformative experience. Interestingly, he gives imitation a significant place in his vision of a "purified religion."

---

20. Alfred N. Whitehead, "Religious Psychology of the Western Peoples." *Whitehead Research.* Accessed January 3, 2023. http://whiteheadresearch.org/occasions/whitehead-reading-group/religious-psychology/.

21. Whitehead. *Religion in the Making,* 56.

In a communal religion you study the will of God in order that He may preserve you; in a purified religion...you study his goodness in order to be like him. It is the difference between the enemy you conciliate and the companion whom you imitate.[22]

Girard's insights can complete things that Whitehead intuited in his thought but did not fully develop. The same is true the other way around as well. Girard goes on to say more about the imitation of Christ or Christlike models than Whitehead does, for instance, though those ideas might map onto Whitehead's conception of God as an ultimate source of desire. For Girard, here we have the ultimate solution to the human problem—to join in participation with a fully non-violent, non-acquisitive model.

Key Theological Implications

Open and relational theology, a phrase coined by theologian Thomas Oord, is a category well suited to include the theological ideas common to both mimetic theory and process philosophy. Whereas many theologies emphasize the absolute changelessness of God, open and relational theology considers love, rather than changelessness, to be of primary value.[23] A God of love implies a certain vulnerability, an openness to affect, and be affected by, relationship.

---

22. Ibid., 40.

23. Thomas Oord identifies the main characteristic of open theology as the pursuit of the logic of love. See Oord, Thomas J., In *Creation Made Free: Open Theology Engaging Science,* (essay, Pickwick Publications, 2009), 28. Jonathan Foster also explores mimetic theory from an open and relational theological perspective. See Foster, Jonathan, *Theology of Consent: Mimetic Theory in an Open and Relational Universe,* (Grasmere, ID: SacraSage, 2022).

"Openness" refers to both the uncontrolling nature of God and the freedom of the world.[24] In a universe where freedom is real and God is love, the world finds itself at liberty to creatively participate in its own becoming. Love and freedom lay the foundation of a relationship between God and the cosmos that is mutually affecting. Such a vision of relationship stands in stark contrast to a view in which God determines every event. Violence and force are not acceptable norms where love is of supreme value, for love persuades rather than forces, influences rather than demands, and seduces rather than controls. An open and relational God doesn't enforce their will from the outside but instead is present in every event, opening possibilities and luring it toward beauty.

We can't overestimate the value of understanding the reality of our violent past, yet having a vibrant hope that our world is pulled forward by beauty. The realism of mimetic theory doesn't have to exclude the hopeful anticipation inherent in process philosophy, nor does process philosophy necessarily suffer from naivety. Joining these narratives together opens a vision of the future: we need not be blind to the reality of our past, but can see the beauty possible for us despite the difficult road that brought us here. Yes, the human capacity for violence can be shocking, but we can use our capacities creatively for the good of our world as well.

In addition, I would say we have the assurance of a loving God who never stops believing the best about us and drawing us forward toward beauty. Process philosophy presents us with a universe oriented towards the value and beauty in the very mind of God: here we have a beautiful and hopeful cosmology. Our anthropological history, articulated by Girard, further assures us that God has made

---

24. The *world* refers to the current actualized order of things. As such it includes the cosmos.

known God's good intentions in the person of Jesus Christ. Both Girard and Whitehead recognize the significance of Jesus from their unique perspectives. Jesus, fully human, provides us with a mimetic model of the co-creativity that is possible for each of us. In the event of Jesus Christ, we see what is possible when a human says yes to the beauty in the mind of God; when flesh welcomes "Logos"—the divine logic.

For both Whitehead and Girard, God is active in human history. Whitehead develops a perspective that shows the immanence of God in every occasion, influencing it toward goodness and beauty. Girard sees the intelligence of God most clearly revealed in Jesus. Mimetic theory and process philosophy share not only conceptual correlations and similar narrative structures, but a similar message: they give us a vision of God and reality we can truly call open and relational. They can be harmonized to create a new level of understanding beyond that offered by each of them alone. And this opens up a whole range of new theological and philosophical possibilities which are only the beginning of a fruitful collaboration in describing an open and relational universe.

Bibliography

Adams, Rebecca J. "Loving Mimesis and Girard's 'Scapegoat of the Text': A Creative Reassessment of Mimetic Desire." In *Violence Renounced: René Girard, Biblical Studies, and Peacemaking*, edited by Willard M. Swartley, 277-307. Telford, PA: Pandora Press U.S., 2000.

Adler, Julius, and Wing-Wai Tse. 1974. "Decision-Making in Bacteria." *Science* 184 (June 21): 1292–1294.

Alison, James, and Wolfgang Palaver. *The Palgrave Handbook of Mimetic Theory and Religion*. New York: Palgrave Macmillan, 2017.

Antonello, Pierpaolo and Gifford, Paul. *How We Became Human: Mimetic Theory and the Science of Evolutionary Origins* (Studies in Violence, Mimesis, & Culture). Michigan State University Press, Kindle Edition, 2015.

Auxier, Randall E. and Herstein, L. Gary. *Quantum of Explanation: Whitehead's Radical Empiricism*. Routledge, 2019.

Bartlett, Anthony. *Theology Beyond Metaphysics: Transformative Semiotics of René Girard*. Cascade Books, Kindle Edition, 2020.

Bradford Wallack F. The Epochal Nature of Process in Whitehead's Metaphysics. Albany: State University of New York Press, 1980.

Burkert, Walter, René Girard, Jonathan Z. Smith, Robert Hamerton-Kelly, and Renato Rosaldo. *Violent origins*. California: Stanford University Press, 1999.

Collins, Robin. "Nature as a Source of Non-Conflictual Desire." In *René Girard and Creative Mimesis*, ed. Vern Neufeld Redekop and Thomas Ryba, 289-312. Lanham, MD: Lexington, 2014.

Chalmers, D. J. Facing up to the problem of consciousness. *Journal of Consciousness Studies* 2: 200-19. 1995.

Dawson, David. *Flesh Becomes Word: A Lexicography of the Scapegoat or, the History of an Idea.* Michigan State University Press, 2013.

Davis, A. M. *Mind, Value, and Cosmos. On the Relational Nature of Ultimacy.* Rowman & Littlefield Publ., 2021.

Eastman, Timothy E., and Hank Keeton. *Physics and Whitehead: Quantum, Process, and Experience.* Albany: State University of New York Press, Kindle Edition, 2004.

Epperson, Michael. *Quantum Mechanics: And the Philosophy of Alfred North Whitehead.* Fordham University Press, Kindle Edition, 2019.

Fleming, Chris., *René Girard: Violence and Mimesis.* Cambridge: Polity Press, 2004.

Faber, Roland. *The Mind of Whitehead: Adventure in Ideas* (p. 85). Pickwick Publications, an imprint of Wipf and Stock Publishers. Kindle Edition.

F. Leron Shults. *Reforming Theological Anthropology: After the Philosophical Turn to Relationality.* Grand Rapids, MI: W.B. Eerdmans, Kindle Edition, 2003.

Foster, Jonathan, *Theology of Consent: Mimetic Theory in an Open and Relational Universe,* Grasmere, ID: SacraSage, 2022.

Goodhart, Sandor, Jørgen Jørgensen, Tom Ryba, and James Williams. *For René Girard: Essays in Friendship and in Truth.* East Lansing: Michigan State University Press, 2012.

Garrels, S. R. Imitation, mirror neurons, and mimetic desire: Convergence between the mimetic theory of René Girard and empirical research on imitation. *Contagion: Journal of Violence, Mimesis, and Culture*, 12 (1), 47–86, 2005. https://doi.org/10.1353/ctn.0.0004

Garrels, S. R. *Mimesis and Science: Empirical research on imitation and the mimetic theory of culture and religion.* East Lansing: Michigan State University Press, 2011.

Girard, René, and Benoît Chantre. *Battling to the End: Conversations with Benoît Chantre.* East Lansing: Michigan State University Press, 2010.

Girard, R. *Deceit, Desire, and the Novel: Self and Other in Literary Structure.* Baltimore: The Johns Hopkins University Press, 2010.

Girard, René. *I See Satan Fall like Lightning.* Ossining, NY: Orbis Books, 2012.

Girard, René. *Evolution and Conversion: Dialogues on the Origins of Culture.* (Bloomsbury Revelations). Bloomsbury Publishing. Kindle Edition, 2017.

Girard, René. *Je Vois Satan Tomber Comme L'éclair.* Paris: Grasset, 2016.

Girard, René. *The Scapegoat,* trans. Yvonne Freccero. Baltimore: The Johns Hopkins University Press, 1986.

Girard, René. *Things Hidden Since the Foundation of the World.* London: Bloomsbury Academic, 2016.

Girard, René. *Violence and the Sacred,* trans. Patrick Gregory. Baltimore: John Hopkins University Press, 1977.

Girard, René. "Violence, Difference, Sacrifice: An Interview with René Girard." Interviewed by Rebecca Adams. In *Violence, Difference, Sacrifice: A Special Issue of Religion and Literature* 25 no. 2 (Summer 1993), ed. Rebecca Adams, 11-33. Reprinted in *René Girard: Prophet of Envy,* ed. Cynthia Haven, 51-72. New York: Bloomsbury Academic, 2020.

Griffin, D. *Animal Minds.* Chicago: University of Chicago Press, 2013.

Griffin, David Ray. *Unsnarling the World-Knot: Consciousness, Freedom, and the Mind-Body Problem.* Eugene, OR: Wipf and Stock Publishers, 2007.

Hartshorne, Charles. *Creative Experiencing: A Philosophy of Freedom.* Ed. Donald Wayne Viney and Jincheal O. Albany, NY: SUNY Press, 2012.

Hartshorne, Charles, "Whitehead in Historical Context," in Charles Hartshorne & W. Creighton Peden, *Whitehead's View of Reality,* UK: Cambridge Scholar Publishing, 2010.

Haught, J. F. *The New Cosmic Story: Inside Our Awakening Universe.* New Haven: Yale University Press. Kindle Edition, 2017.

Haven, Cynthia L. *Evolution of Desire* (Studies in Violence, Mimesis, & Culture). East Lansing: Michigan State University Press, Kindle Edition, 2018.

Heim, S. M. *Saved From Sacrifice: A Theology of the Cross.* Grand Rapids, MI: Eerdmans, 2008.

Heisenberg, Werner. *Physics and Beyond*. London: Allen & Unwin, 1981.

https://violenceandreligion.com/.

Jones, Judith A. *Intensity: An Essay in Whiteheadian Ontology*. Nashville, TN: Vanderbilt University Press, 1998.

Kirwan, Michael. *Girard and Theology*. London: T & T Clark, 2009.

Kirwan, Michael and Sheelah T. Hidden, eds. *Mimesis and Atonement: René Girard and the Doctrine of Salvation*. London: Bloomsbury Academic, 2018.

Kraus, Elizabeth. *The Metaphysics of Experience* (American Philosophy) New York: Fordham University Press. Kindle Edition, 2018

Lemaire, Anika. *Jacques Lacan*, trans. David Macey. Abington, UK: Routledge, 1991.

Maria-Teresa Teixeira, Aljoscha Berve and Moirika Reker, eds. *Mind in Nature: Bridging Process Philosophy and Neoplatonism*. Newcastle upon Tyne: Cambridge Scholars Publishing, 2021.

Marion, Jean-Luc, and Stephen E. Lewis. *The Erotic Phenomenon*. Chicago: The University of Chicago Press, 2008.

Meltzoff, Andrew N., and M. Keith Moore. "Explaining Facial imitation: A Theoretical Model." *Infant and Child Development* 6, no. 3-4, 1997.

Mesle, C. Robert. *Process-Relational Philosophy*. Conshohocken, PA: Templeton Press, 2008.

Oord, Thomas. J. *Creation Made Free: Open Theology Engaging Science*. Eugene, OR: Pickwick Publications, 2009.

Oord, Thomas. J. *Pluriform Love: An Open and Relational Theology of Well-Being*. Grasmere, ID: SacraSage Press, 2022.

Oord. Thomas. J. *The Uncontrolling Love of God: An Open and Relational Account of Providence*. Downers Grove, Illinois: Intervarsity Press, 2015.

Oughourlian, Jean-Michel, and Eugene Webb. *The Genesis of Desire*. East Lansing: Michigan State University Press, 2010.

Oughourlian, Jean-Michel. *The Mimetic Brain* (Studies in Violence, Mimesis, & Culture). East Lansing: Michigan State University Press, Kindle Edition, 2016

Porphyry. *On Aristotle Categories*, trans. Steven K. Strange. London: Blooms-bury, 2014.

Rescher, Nicholas. *Process Metaphysics: An Introduction to Process Philosophy*. Albany: State University of New York Press, 1996.

Robinson, Howard, "Dualism," *The Stanford Encyclopedia of Philosophy*, Edward N. Zalta, ed., https://plato.stanford.edu/archives/fall2020/entries/dualism/

Russell. *Philosophical Essays for Alfred North Whitehead*. New York: Russell & Russell, 1936.

Ryba, Thomas, and Vern Neufeld Redekop, eds. *René Girard and Creative Mimesis*. Lanham, MD: Lexington Books, 2014.

Vanheeswijck, Guy. "The Place of René Girard in Contemporary Philosophy." *Contagion: Journal of Violence, Mimesis, and Culture*. doi:10.1353/ctn.2003.0004.

Viney, Donald W., and Shields, George. W. *The Mind of Charles Hartshorne: A Critical Examination*. Anoka, MN: Process Century Press, 2020.

Ward, Keith. *Rational Theology and the Creativity of God*. Oxford: Basil Blackwell, 1985.

Weber, Michel and Anderson Weekes. *Process Approaches to Consciousness in Psychology, Neuroscience, and Philosophy of Mind*. Albany, NY: SUNY Press, Kindle Edition, 2011.

Weber, Michel and Will Desmond, eds. *Handbook of Whiteheadian Process Thought, Volume 1*. Frankfurt / Lancaster: ontos verlag, Process Thought X1 & X2, 2008.

Weber, Michel and Will Desmond, eds. *Handbook of Whiteheadian Process Thought, Volume 2*. Frankfurt / Lancaster: ontos verlag, Process Thought X1 & X2, 2008.

Whitehead, Alfred. N. *Adventures of ideas*. New York: Free Press, 2010.

Whitehead, Alfred. N. *Modes of Thought*. New York: Free Press, 2010.

Whitehead, Alfred. N. *Religion in the Making: Lowell Lectures, 1926*. Cambridge: Cambridge University Press, 2011.

Whitehead, Alfred. N. "Religious Psychology of the Western Peoples." *Whitehead Research*. Accessed January 3, 2023. http://whiteheadresearch. org/occasions/whitehead-reading-group/religious-psychology/.

Whitehead, Alfred. N. *Science and the Modern World*. New York: Open Road Media, 2021.

Whitehead, Alfred. N. *Symbolism, Its Meaning and Effect: Barbour-Page Lectures, University of Virginia, 1927*. New York: Fordham University Press, 1985.

Whitehead, Alfred. N. *Process and Reality* (Gifford Lectures Delivered in the University of Edinburgh During the Session 1927-28). New York: Free Press, Kindle Edition, 1979.

Whitehead, Alfred. N. *The Function of Reason*. Baltimore, MD: Agora Publications. Kindle Edition. 2014.

Index